WALK A MILE IN MY SHOES

A Book about Biological Parents
for Foster Parents
and Social Workers

Judith A.B. Lee, D.S.W.
Danielle Nisivoccia, D.S.W.

Child Welfare League of America • Washington, DC

Walk A Mile in My Shoes is published in collaboration with the Center for the Study of Child Welfare, The University of Connecticut, School of Social Work, West Hartford, CT.

CHILD WELFARE LEAGUE OF AMERICA, INC.
440 First Street, NW, Suite 310, Washington, DC 20001-2085

CURRENT PRINTING (last digit)
10 9 8 7 6 5 4 3 2

Cover design by Anita Crouch
Text design by Eve Malakoff-Klein

Printed in the United States of America

ISBN # 0-87868-349-6

Dedicated
to the memories of
Anne M. Beach and Rosalie Myers,
our mothers,
who met the challenges and loved us well.

CONTENTS

FOREWORD

Walk a Mile in My Shoes addresses an important need in the field of child welfare. Although much of this book is written in a way that speaks directly to foster parents, it is equally valuable for child welfare workers and associated staff. Biological parents may also discover certain segments to be helpful in their own situations. As an "old dyed-in-the-wool" public welfare worker, I found that this work resonated deeply with my own previous direct practice experiences. It also makes it very clear that child welfare practice has become much more difficult and complex, making this book a welcome addition to the child welfare literature. The University of Connecticut School of Social Work is pleased to have had a small part in this effort.

Written in an easily readable, unpretentious, jargon-free style, Walk a Mile in My Shoes clearly yet eloquently captures the subtle and profound difficulties associated with the foster care service system. Speaking to the treatment team consisting of worker and foster parent and recognizing the sometimes competing pressures and interests in our present resource-poor environment, the authors address both the problems, dilemmas, and frequent opportunities for success in the foster care arrangement.

The "shoes" that are worn in this book are those of the biological parent, the least understood actor in the foster care triad. Despite being the least understood, biological parents are crucial to a positive outcome. Workers and foster parents need help in struggling and coming to grips with their feelings of anger, pity, sorrow, compassion, and other often conflicting feelings about biological parents. Facing up to these feelings are necessary if the delicate lattice of human relationships and interactions are to be woven together to successfully result in a permanent living arrangement in the best interest of the child. The authors both instruct and encourage people to explore their feelings, which if not addressed, could interfere with the helping process in the foster care relationship. While the biological parent is the central focus, this work clearly illustrates the position and struggles of the child welfare worker and foster parent as well, thereby enabling each to better understand the world of the other. Using case vignettes which could easily lend themselves to teaching or training tools, the authors are able to powerfully demonstrate both the subtle and obvious dilemmas faced by each set of actors in the foster care triad.

The authors note that their work has been informed by the ecological perspective and acknowledge the contributions of Carel Germain. Useful in all social service settings, the ecological perspective is particularly so in child welfare service systems where the transactions between people and their environments and the intricate interactions among the various participants can best be explored and judged using the "goodness of fit" criteria. Drawing on the works of such major scholars in child welfare as Maluccio, Hartman, Laird, and Jenkins, among others, the authors fashion a down-to-earth, real world discussion of the complex issues present in a way that will allow readers to immediately use and apply the material to their places in the child welfare service enterprise. While not an easy task, particularly when it is done so well, this is an effort that is timely, appreciated, and much needed.

Dr. Nancy A. Humphreys, Dean
University of Connecticut, School of Social Work
Hartford, CT

PREFACE

S ince the original version of this volume was published in 1980, much has happened in the field of child welfare. Such developments as the emphasis on permanency planning for children and youth, the problems and needs of families with children at risk of out-of-home placement, and the substantial proportion of adolescents in foster care have further challenged child welfare agencies and personnel.

As a result, there have been growing demands on foster parents, who are increasingly expected to serve as "professional" members of the service team in public and private agencies. In particular, foster parents more and more need to relate and be of help to birth parents of children in their care. For this reason, the present volume is welcome and exciting.

Dr. Judith A.B. Lee and Dr. Danielle Nisivoccia offer a timely and useful text that will help enhance the central role of foster parents with birth parents and promote the goals and values of permanency planning for children and youth in foster care. We appreciate the authors' contribution, and especially the thought and effort that they devoted to preparing a volume that is strongly knowledge-based as well as relevant for practice. We also thank the Administration for Children, Youth, and Families, U.S. Department of Health and Human Services, for funding our training project, "Toward More Effective Work with Biological Parents," through which the original version of this volume was produced as part of a range of training materials.

Anthony N. Maluccio, Ph.D.
Professor and Director
Center for the Study of Child Welfare
University of Connecticut, School of Social Work
Hartford, CT

ACKNOWLEDGMENTS

We are especially grateful to Dr. Carel B. Germain, whose seminal work on the ecological perspective in social work guides our thinking and whose encouragement and wisdom immeasurably enriches our lives.

We also thank Rose Gutman, M.S.W., who was our director and a role model of practice excellence at the Division of Foster Home Care and Adoption Services, Special Services to Children, New York City. Later Deputy Director, Office of Direct Child Care Services of the Human Resources Administration, and now retired, she remains our consultant, inspiration, and dear friend.

We acknowledge the support of Dean Nancy A. Humphreys and Dr. Anthony N. Maluccio, and the University of Connecticut School of Social Work Center for the Study of Child Welfare. We especially thank Mrs. Virginia Starkie, whose typing and instrumental and emotional support made this book possible.

Finally, we acknowledge the commitment of the foster parents and workers we have known. This approach to children and their families rests in their able hands and in the shared dream of a more humane society with social and distributive justice for all.

INTRODUCTION

The placement of children in foster family care is a temporary helping measure usually brought about by an emergency situation. It is a drastic action to assure the safety and well-being of children when the environment in the child's own home is not conducive to meeting these basic needs.[1] It is hoped that every effort to sustain the child at home would have been made before placement, for we know that children have strong and critically important attachments to their families no matter how much trouble the family is having.

Why are children placed? We need a way of understanding what happens when families are in such severe trouble that children must be removed for their protection and safety. Our understanding is influenced by our view of the world. In the early days of child placement, the world view was static—a cause-and-effect one. Children were seen as victims to be rescued from bad parents and bad environments before they too "turned bad." City children were taken from their parents and sent out West.[2] Families were broken up because parents were seen as the only cause of their own difficulties. There was no thought of reuniting the family or of broken attachments and broken hearts. Children were "bound out" or indentured as apprentices. Some were placed in orphanages. There was also an economic aspect to breaking up families. Under the shadow of teaching children to be self-sufficient and removing them from evil influences (their parents), the need for free labor was met.[3] Though this type of "child saving" ended later in the 19th century, these moralistic ideas persisted well into the 20th century. In every sphere of life, including science, medicine, and social work, thinking was cause and effect. The latter 20th century eventually brought a new kind of thinking, as medicine and science caught up with the complexity of the times. If there was any causality of events, it was seen as immeasurable multicausality. "General systems" theory advanced the ideas of the interdependence of all parts, or that a breakdown in any one part could affect other parts. In the late 1960s these ideas evolved in social work as well, but it has been hard for social workers to let go of the early medical model cause-and-effect thinking.[4]

Carel Germain's application of concepts from human ecology to social work provides us with a perspective that helps us view the transactions between people and their environments in their complexity. People are in continual transaction with the physical and social/economic/political environments all around them. When the transactions are good enough— a "goodness of fit"— people and environments gain in competence, autonomy, self-direction, relatedness, and identity or self-esteem. When the transactions are not good enough, people and environments suffer. Environments may be noxious, polluted, non-nutritive, and hardly able to sustain life. People can affect and be affected by noxious environments.[5]

If you think of people at the seashore on a beautiful clear day, then of massive debris washing ashore; or of the pollution of our air; or of a large body of polluted water, with plant and marine life dying; or even of a fish tank with its filter broken; you will have a visual image of the ecological perspective. In the social sense, poverty, uneven opportunities for work and education, stigma, racism, sexism, and other discriminations are pollutions as well. The biological family's struggles must be viewed in the context of this ecological perspective. It is obvious then that a balance in lives and environments must be restored and that the problems precipitating child placement are always bigger than individual inadequacy in parenting. In their book *Permanency Planning for Children*, Anthony Maluccio and his colleagues state that the ecological perspective should be adopted as a framework for working with parents and children, as well as for understanding their lives.[6]

For example, in our ecological understanding of child

placement, we know that the "hard services" necessary to sustain family life are, at best, unevenly provided. These services include adequate financial security to provide for material needs, and housing.[7] Families with children are increasing dramatically among the now three and a half million homeless in this nation.[8] Affordable housing is often lacking, causing extra stress that adds to family breakdown and child placement. "Soft services" to keep children at home are also often lacking, such as day care and flexible, reaching-out counseling. In reality we cannot often say that sufficient at-home services have been provided to prevent placement.[9]

This is further complicated by the fact that in this society the poor, the mentally or physically challenged, the mentally ill, women, minorities of color, gay people, and others who are different and carry stigma have more difficulty in gaining access to the resources and services that may exist. Any cutback in funding of human resources supports remedial measures at best. Yet those involved in efforts to reunify families once children are placed know all too well that resources for this task are not allotted. Services are equally difficult to obtain before or after placement. Placement can provide safety and security to children but at the expense of profound loss, severed attachments, stigma, and major painful transitions for all family members, and most critically for the children we are trying to protect.

These days, most foster children are in care under court order (73%), and most parents therefore see their children placed in foster care involuntarily.[10] Federal law now mandates that children in foster care not be left "in limbo"; that agencies are accountable for permanency planning reviews every six months; and that a permanent plan be realized for children within 18 months. This plan might be family reunification, termination of parental rights and adoption, or long-term care and independent living. Nationally, 75% of the foster children are returned home, but one study points out that 32% of them return to care.[11] The lack of basic services no doubt contributes to this reentry phenomenon. Eighteen months is an eternity in a child's sense of time, but very short when one considers the complex problems bringing children into care and the lack of basic resources.

Whether or not the permanent plan is to return home, the child and family must be helped to preserve their attachments. In this complex ecological field, the tasks of the foster care agency, worker, foster parent, biological parent, and child are recognized as extremely difficult, perhaps more difficult than ever before in history. These actors are the frontline team in an immense undertaking. They each deserve recognition and support in taking on tasks of this magnitude.

Sometimes when such hard tasks are demanded, team members may fall to blaming each other—most often the parent—for problems or obstacles to resolution. Outside agencies without an ecological perspective also blame these actors instead of understanding the complex interplay of forces that include the current economic and political conditions. That is why it is so important to recognize that the ecological realities make it almost impossible for the tasks to be carried out easily. Basic changes in the way this society provides for human needs are needed to prevent placements and to facilitate reunification. Casting blame on any member of the team is a tragic error. Workers, foster parents, and biological parents are all to be credited with doing their best with the difficult task of putting Humpty Dumpty, the broken family unit, back together again.

Most workers, foster parents, and biological parents we have have known in our 22 years of practice in foster care were compassionate, hardworking, more than adequate, and well motivated. Many were also angry and frustrated. As one foster mother said in bitter tears on a discharge day: "It's the poverty. I hate to see her go back to the poverty. What I gave her and what her mother gives her may not stand against this cancerous poverty. I know firsthand, I barely made it out of poverty myself."

As poverty has grown, so has child maltreatment.[12] Although the federal policies regarding permanency planning did bring about a reduction in the number of children in foster care, the trend is again rising as poverty, drug addiction, and lack of housing increase.[13] Abuse and neglect occur across all lines, but poor families face continual and inordinate pressures that make the tasks and timetable of reunification so much more difficult. Maltreatment and poverty are clearly connected. The rate for all forms of maltreatment was highest for cases with annual incomes less than $7,000. Seventy-nine percent of the cases reported for physical abuse had incomes under $15,000; 91% of the cases reported for physical neglect had incomes under $15,000.[14] This no doubt reflects the exceptional tensions and stresses poor people face, as well as the fact that abuse and neglect of poor children tends to be reported more than maltreatment in higher socioeconomic groups.[15]

Joan Laird describes the foster care dilemma: "In a system of gross economic inequality, is it right that weaker groups should be systematically deprived first of their ability to make a living and then of the children they are unable to support? But are we to abandon children who are victims of poverty and abuse while we wait for society-wide solutions to massive social problems? On the other hand, how much will it postpone needed social and economic changes if we continue to temporize with second-best or ad hoc solutions?"[16]

Until the causes and effects of poverty are properly dealt with, we do the best we can for children and families caught in oppressive systems. This book addresses the important work that individual team members can do person-to-person, while we work in society at large for equal opportunity and the basic human needs of us all. This book is intended to help workers and foster parents embrace the complexity of the situation and develop the skills to help biological families remain attached. This may be one of the hardest tasks on earth, complicated by a lack of resources and at times ethical dilemmas as well.

Charles Levy reminds us of the ethical element: "The ethical issues that arise in the social worker's practice usually cannot be resolved without contending with a multiplicity of diverse, sometimes conflicting interests. A child's interests may not coincide with the interests of his [sic] parents, and yet the interests of both may merit the social worker's earnest ethical consideration."[17]

We cannot simplify the intricate and interrelated problems encountered in keeping biological families together, but we can try to get into the shoes of biological parents and from that perspective learn what is necessary to restore ties. We hope that this book will develop empathy and knowledge about biological parents in workers and foster parents so that they might work effectively as a team in preserving the ties of biological parents and children whatever the permanent plan may be. Foster parents may use it as a self-help guide, and workers may use it to attune themselves to the tasks both foster and biological parents face. It may be used by agencies in the separate and joint training of workers and foster parents, and by teachers and students in learning about biological families.

1

THE FRONTLINE TEAM

F oster family care is the child welfare service that provides full-time substitute care for children when their
own families cannot care for them for a temporary or
extended period.[18] The mission of foster care agencies is to
reunite the family or to plan for adoption. To make a plan for
a placed child is a difficult task for all involved. Although the
workers in a foster care agency have a particular function
and role, the way they carry them out together in making a
permanent plan for a foster child is crucial. The workers,
while having the children as their main focus, must be
equally attentive to the biological parents and the foster
parents. Each person in the triad—the child, the biological
parent, and the foster parent—should be in harmony, working on the plan. The frontline team then consists of the
worker, backed by the supervisor and administration of the
agency, the foster family, the biological family, and the child
when he or she is mature enough to take part. All members
of the team are vital in the common effort.

THE WORKER

The worker is responsible for mediating, negotiating and
advocating for all the persons in the triad, while at the same
time remaining objective. This is a tall order.

The social work Code of Ethics expects the social worker
to respect the worth, rights, dignity, and self-determination
of clients. At the same time, the worker is a person from a
particular cultural background and socioeconomic class,
with its values and assumptions. As Levy notes, "The social
worker's professional ethics must transcend his [sic] per-

sonal ethics when the two are not entirely reconcilable. For this purpose, he needs to be aware of his own values and behavioral preferences, including those that arise out of his social, economic, and religious identification."[19] There may be a clash of the worker's personal values and professional values. This can result in tension and conflict for the social worker, and in possibly siding with one member of the triad at the expense of another.

The conflicting values of many social institutions contribute, both overtly and covertly, to the continuing tension between the members of the team. It is not only the worker's values that enter into her or his work with the triad, but the contradictory values of the socioeconomic and political institutions of society.

The task of the social worker in foster care is an excellent prototype of the function of the social worker as described by William Schwartz: "To mediate the process through which individuals and their systems reach out to each other....More specifically...in a complex and often disordered society, the individual-social symbiosis grows diffuse and obscure in varying degrees...to where that attachment appears to be all but severed."[20] In the noxious environments where biological families must try to survive are many examples of these "almost severed" ties between people and their systems. At all points along this range, the social work function is to mediate the individual-social transaction as it is worked out in the context of specific agencies.

The role of the worker in foster care is, then, to mediate between the child and the biological parent, the child and the foster family; the child and all relevant systems such as health care and schools, courts, and the agency itself; and between the biological parent and the child; the biological parent and the foster parent; the biological parent and all other systems needed to restore the family to full functioning and reunification, such as the legal system, finances, housing, medical and counseling, hard and soft services, including the agency itself.

Seeing the worker's function as mediation— "to act as agent in bringing, effecting, or communicating" [Webster]— is helpful, as is the knowledge that the worker's task is not that of a magician to make everything all better. Neither is the task to change people or to change the system (far too grandiose tasks, at best), "but to change the way in which they deal with each other".[21] It helps to recognize that the social work function is necessarily circumscribed within several activities. Maluccio, and his colleagues[22] point out five: case planning, case management, therapy, client advocacy, and court witness.

According to Germain and Gitterman, people, including children in placement and their families, have problems in living in three interrelated spheres of life: the transitional (including developmental), the interpersonal, and the environmental spheres.[23] Foster care social workers therefore also have to be, at times, teacher, enabler, facilitator, resource broker, and advocate, as well as mediator. Acting as frontline team member and as team leader are the critical roles, but the activities may overlap and may also be carried out by more than one worker, so that careful case coordination is necessary. The permanency planning process requires decisive, assertive, and compassionate social work.[24] Most workers will find themselves carrying out several roles.

THE FOSTER FAMILY

Foster parents are very special people. They have decided to provide care for children whose parents are not able to care for them. They have entered a special relationship with children, their biological parents, and the agency, sharing rights and responsibilities. They are pivotal members of a helping team working together toward the goal of helping the child and permanency planning. They bear the burden of a 24-hour per day commitment.

Foster parenthood requires a new kind of parenting— to have for a while yet not to keep; to love but not exclusively; to help children and their parents to maintain their ties. It is an unselfish love— directed more toward the other person than toward oneself. Foster parents are rare people who feel they can help a child without exclusive rights. This kind of giving of oneself is not easy. Foster families have all the qualities of all families and parents, but they are team members, too. They are offering a family-caregiving service to children and their families. They bring their own solid parenting experience to the task, but they have also learned the particular aspects of foster parenting, and helping children and families to remain attached.

One of the hardest things in foster parenting is working out the relationship with the biological parents. When Johnny or Jean comes back upset from a visit with his or her parents, or silent and sullen, foster parents may have second thoughts. They may feel "I do all the work" and "she gets all the pleasure and love from the child," or "why does the agency permit and encourage these visits when the child gets so upset?" or "why isn't she nicer to me? I do my best for her child." These are painful, understandable human feelings, yet even more is asked of foster parents: to understand and try to help the very persons who seem to hurt the children. Patience, warmth, and understanding of biological parents are essential "tools of the trade."

Social and economic institutions value foster parents more highly than biological parents, particularly in the tremendous difference in foster care and welfare payments, though neither is sufficient to the task and foster parents often give of their own funds to supplement the foster care payments. Foster parents may become a vital support system for biological parents, but in practice this is difficult because of the unequal societal values attached to the two families. Foster parents may be held up to biological parents as ideal and more worthwhile. Biological parents may find it hard to reach out to the foster family for these reasons. Foster parents must demonstrate genuine acceptance of and respect for biological families if foster parents are to become a support system.

Once foster parents have succeeded in really understanding the child's parents, it will not be as difficult a situation, for "understanding and tolerance are twin sisters."[25] The ability to help follows close behind. Evelyn Felker, a foster parent herself, has developed the principle that foster parents should "play second fiddle" to the biological parents, and that they "must support the efforts of the parent to be a parent."[26] Yet this is often hard to do. It is often easier to judge another than to understand.

An old Indian proverb asks us not to judge others before we walk a mile in their shoes. Let us walk this mile together and deepen our understanding of the parents whose children are placed in foster care. Who are these parents? How do they feel? Why do they let it happen? How can foster parents help? How can the frontline team work together?

When children become a part of the foster family, they bring their own family with them actually and in memory. They now have two sets of parents—a potential source of conflict, with children feeling pulled by divided loyalties. The children can have attachments to both sets of parents without having to choose between them if foster parents are able to develop a relationship of respect, understanding, and concern toward the biological family.

The foster family has been approved to care for foster children by an agency that values highly their parenting ability. What would it be like to be in the shoes of the biological parents? What would it feel like to have an agency tell you that for now you are not able to care for your child—that someone else has to take over? What would it feel like to see your child go off with a social worker to an unknown place? You would say "but I would never let it happen!" but here are some questions that have to be thought about: how would you feel about yourself, your child, the agency, the foster parents? How would you handle these feelings? What would it take and who would help you gain the strength to get your child back?

THE CHILD

Children of all ages, races, religions, socioeconomic classes, and family backgrounds enter foster care. In 1983, 53% were male and 52.7% were white. Thirty-four percent were black and 7.3% were Hispanic.[27] In the 1950s and early 1960s, foster parents who preferred infants, toddlers, or early-school-age children had some chance of having such a child placed. Children entered care earlier and stayed longer. Services to prevent placement, reunify families and preserve attachments were uneven at best. By 1977, however, the average age of children in foster care was 10.8 years old, and by 1983 it was 12.6 years old.[28] Older children bring complex histories and often special needs into foster care.

In 1983, 79% of the children were placed through the

courts because of parental abuse or neglect. An additional 11.2% had parental rights terminated, and 5.8% were placed voluntarily by their parents.[29] Children entering care after experiencing abusive or neglectful situations need special understanding, especially regarding the complexity of their feelings for their parents. Although they may feel abandoned, frightened, angry, withdrawn, sad, and ambivalent, most cling to their attachment to their parents. They need help to sort out their feelings and work out safe, useful relationships with their parents while receiving nurturance and help from the foster family. The ability of each foster child's two families to work together toward these goals is critical in putting broken lives back together again.

Most children have an array of reactions to placement that are usually subconscious.[30] Good preparation of the children before placement, and early follow-up after placement, can do a great deal of good. They may feel: rejection, which engenders feelings of worthlessness; guilt, which leads children to think they have contributed to breaking up the home; hostility, which reinforces the guilt, because hostile feelings, particularly against one's own parents, are a punishable offense; fear of abandonment; fear of the unknown; shame.

Services such as counseling, individually and in children's or teen groups; psychotherapy when needed; remedial and enriched education; and a good range of competence-building, leisure-time activities are also helpful. Family counseling for children together with their biological families may help. In addition, the children need to know that everything possible is being done to help their parents reestablish their lives and home.

Children who have been physically and/or sexually abused also need to have safety guaranteed through the careful monitoring of visiting plans. Although visiting for most children should be frequent to preserve and rework positive ties, children who are fearful of visiting should be listened to carefully. In some cases, visiting will be prohibited for a period of time. In cases of sexual abuse, children may need to be assured that the offending parent has received treatment before seeing the child again. Children need to know that parents are being helped to change abusive behavior, and that it is not disloyal to protect themselves when frightened by signs that the behavior may recur, as when parents begin to drink, or argue with each other violently. The older child can be helped to report this behavior, to seek help, and to say no.[31]

The atmosphere for open communication in these taboo areas must be established. Children must be able to talk to workers, foster parents, and their parents directly about abusive behavior, and about what they as children need from their point of view, to return home. In that sense, children are the critical part of the permanent planning process. They are not responsible for the plans, but they must be empowered to speak up about their own needs.

It is also important to come to grips with our own feelings about the child and the parent/offender when children have been sexually abused. Unexamined feelings about the parties involved will inevitably be conveyed in some way and will interfere with the help that one is trying to give. The key to dealing with such difficult situations is to make all of the feelings talkable, starting with our own.

Children must be able to talk about the various aspects of their lives that, added together, form their identity. "Who am I? Where do I come from? Where am I going?" are critical questions in the lives of all foster children. According to Joan Laird, despite the "nurturing goodness of substitute care, the child's ongoing task will always be to reweave the jagged tear in the fabric of his [sic] identity, to make himself whole again."[32] If a worker or foster parent is in conflict about a child's own family, the child knows it and self-esteem falls accordingly. We must help the child "mend the jagged tear" as we seek harmony in working with the child's family.

THE BIOLOGICAL PARENTS

The primary reason why children come into foster care is found in family breakdown or incapacity, exacerbated by severe environmental pressures.[33] The breakdown of the family may be the result of one or a multitude of combined individual and environmental problems, poverty foremost among them. A minimal 1988 estimate of the correlation between poverty and placement is that the families of 37% of the children placed would have been eligible for AFDC funds. This does not take into account children of poor working families and is therefore an extremely low estimate.[34]

Political and philosophical agreement is lacking as to the relationship of the government to the family in general. There is no national policy for all families. Although Americans aspire to a belief in the virtues of the family and home, we have no guaranteed universal basic income or services for families. Perhaps our national values are geared toward the self-sufficient family, and the covert message is that a financially dependent family is not a worthy family and not entitled to a basic good quality of life. As Joan Laird notes, "We seem to believe an AFDC mother deserves less and can support her child on less income than can a foster mother."[35] Biological parents are all too painfully aware of this lack of equality and the connections between poverty and placement.

It is increasingly difficult to be a parent, and the times in which we live contribute greatly to this difficulty. The pressures on single parents, poor parents, young parents, and two-parent working families are enormous, and the supportive resources are highly inadequate for people who are not well-to-do. The sociologist Urie Bronfenbrenner notes that children and parents are more alienated from each other than ever before.[36] Many children may spend no individual time with adults during the day. Even when a supervising adult is available, children may be spending solitary time with machines—TVs, stereos, and computers. This lack of adult-child or even peer interaction is bound to have an effect on the children's sense of relatedness. Latchkey children are often left to fend for themselves while single parents and parents in lower socioeconomic and middle-class families must work long hours and double shifts to make ends meet. Extended families where relatives or close friends are available for child care are increasingly rare in this age of the nuclear family. The undertow of drugs and antisocial activities exists in all communities these days. The tasks of parenting under these conditions are immense. People are not born parents nor is good parenting skill just absorbed naturally. Yet few learning opportunities are available, and parents have little extra time to use what may be in place.

For many of the biological parents, the scene is complicated by other special problems, such as physical or mental illness, serious struggles with family violence and abuse connected with alcoholism or drug addiction, and other exceptional circumstances.

The biological parents are just people who are attempting to parent under extremely trying conditions and amid many obstacles. They need resources and support from all frontline team members and available support networks to achieve effective parenthood and positive attachments to their children. They deserve all the help we can give.

2

MORE ABOUT THE BIOLOGICAL PARENTS

W ho are the biological parents? Why are children placed? Many studies have researched the reasons for placement but since each has used different categories, and most are very general, it is difficult to come up with an overall profile of the biological parent. The best we can do is offer various descriptions.

For example, a 1983 study by Yoshikami and Emlen reported that nationally the placements of 73% of all the children then in care were court-ordered and 25% were placed on a voluntary basis. The reasons given for involuntary placement were child abuse or neglect; the reasons for voluntary placement were parental absence, financial hardship, illness, disability, and substance abuse by parents or children. However, the causes behind the abuse or the neglect of the court-placed children were not given. It is likely that they were similar to the causes of the voluntary placements but were not stated because of the necessity for hard evidence in making statements about court-involved cases, in contrast to voluntary placements.[37]

Another study cites five major reasons that biological parents have to place their children: physical illness or incapacity of the child-caring person, including confinement; mental illness of the mother; personality or emotional problems of the child; severe neglect or abuse; or other family problems, including unwillingness or inability to continue care, desertion, parental incompetence, alcoholism or other addiction, marital conflicts, or arrest.[38]

Sometimes these reasons can combine in a landslide effect; sometimes one reason or another prevails. Poverty can complicate any problem, and cause many. In still another study it was found that more than half of the families placing children were working class, and the financial pressures added by lower incomes compounded the problems greatly.[39] In addition, many others received welfare. For the majority of children and their families, placement is an emergency, an unplanned traumatic experience in the lives of all concerned. As foster mother Evelyn Felker says: "Many [biological] parents are coping with problems beyond the magnitude of anything we have experienced. There are varying degrees of success but I have found much to wonder at and admire."[40]

We turn now to some reasons for placement, illustrating each with a true story to further help us get into the parents' shoes.

REASONS FOR PLACEMENT

Physical Illness

Have you ever been so sick that you needed friends and family to come help out? Whom did you call upon? Who came? What did they do? Did they care for your children? How did you feel about being sick and needing others to help you and your children? Pretty helpless? It can be a frightening situation. Maybe you were fortunate to have people come to your aid while you were getting better.

Physical illness, ranging from diseases like asthma and hepatitis to the need for surgery, complications of pregnancy, and gynecological problems, ranks high on the list of placement emergencies. Today, AIDS has also become a major tragic illness causing the placement of children, particularly infected infants who may be ready medically to leave the hospital but unable to return to a home with ill parents. Many of these children remain in group or institutional care because of the irrational fear of AIDS. Foster parents caring for children with AIDS are exceptional people; they face both societal stigma and probably the eventual death of the child. Physical illness can happen to anyone, but when parents do not have family members or neighbors willing to pitch in and help, children may have to leave home. Most parents who placed their children were ill for at least a year before placement.

Here is a story of a parent who placed children while physically ill. A mother, who was separated from her husband eight months before her illness, said:

> I felt very tired and sick, and I went to a hospital in my neighborhood where they told me I needed to be hospitalized immediately since I had hepatitis. I told them I had no one to take care of my children, and the doctor took me to the hospital social service department. They called the city social service department downtown and the children were placed. I have no friends here and the only one to take care of my children was my mother-in-law and she was in another country. [41]

Mental Illness

Society is harsh on people with mental illness. Words like "crazy" or "incompetent" or "nuts" are thrown like stones at people who have experienced severe problems leading to hospitalization. It is hard to get by those words without examining our own feelings about people so labeled. We may be frightened or anxious in their presence. We may think "it's inherited" and the children have "bad blood."

But have you ever felt lonely and blue? Have you ever felt so nervous that you could not concentrate or perform your daily tasks? Have you ever been in a pressure-cooker situation, when you felt that you would explode if just one more thing happened? All of these are normal feelings. When they are felt suddenly, out of the blue, in the extreme and for long periods of time, a breakdown of ability to cope may result. Pressures can be from within or without. We know, these days, that there are biochemical, organic, and genetic explanations for mental illness and that stress also plays a part. Extreme pressures or crisis situations can be too hard for some people to handle, especially when there are no others to rely upon for help and support. Here are two stories of parents who placed their children while experiencing such severe problems in living.

I had a nervous breakdown and I knew I was not myself. I asked my neighbor to call the police because I was so nervous and confused. My vision was blurred. Everything I touched was colored blue. I was not paying attention to the baby. I would feel sad for long periods of time. My sister committed suicide four years ago so when I began not to feel myself I got help. The police came for the baby.

In many one-parent households, institutionalization of the adult, even temporarily, leads to foster care for the children. A mother reports:

The court sent me to a city hospital for observation. Then I was sent to a state hospital. I got very angry in court because I got tired of going there every few weeks because my husband wouldn't pay the court order. I was tired and nervous and had no money and was taking care of all the children. I told the judge he wasn't treating me fairly....I guess I was shouting at the judge.[42]

Problems of the Child

Sometimes a child is born "different," physically, emotionally, or intellectually. A child with a serious physical impairment or deformity, or a child who does not respond to parental affection (such as an autistic child), or a child born profoundly retarded, can sometimes be too much for a family to handle, particularly when there are other stresses. Sometimes the child's trouble is not evident at birth. For example, emotional problems can show up later.

There might come a point when relatives, friends, neighbors, or teachers bring the child's problems to the parents' attention. Sometimes children begin to act up in school, do not learn, are sullen, withdrawn, or fresh; they may become truant and hang around with "the wrong crowd." As they get older they won't listen and obey, they may fight with parents who are at their wits' end. Family life is horrible. Parents are aware that the situation has become so bad that they can no longer deal with it. With the social worker's help, some parents send their children to special boarding schools or residential treatment centers while others place them in foster homes. The change of climate emotionally as well as socially and physically can be a real help for some children. Here are two stories of placement due to the problems of the child.

My baby was born retarded and without an esophagus. I was 20 and had two children at home. I just couldn't feed the baby although the nurses showed me how to use a feeding tube. It was just too much for me. My husband was more afraid of the baby than I was. He couldn't touch him. My mother was sick herself and couldn't help. The foster mother was helpful. I began to learn from her, but it took me a long time to cope with it.

Another mother reported on the placement of a 13-year-old girl.

She stopped going to school because she seemed unable to attend a function with a large group of people. She has a speech defect....She sounded like Donald Duck and became unhappy and withdrawn because the children teased her. At the same time I broke up with my husband....Then one doctor decided it was her nose and in January she had another operation. She was terrified. In March I moved away from where she lived all her life. I had to get out of that terrible neighborhood. She hated everything about the new apartment and the new school. She hated going to school and in May she stopped and stayed home by herself. She often called me because she was scared. In the summer we moved again and she said she would go to the new school but when she started she said she was too frightened. She went for a month and then started therapy at a city hospital. As soon as she started therapy she stopped going to school. She criticized me and opposed me in every way....Around Christmas she threw things at me, blamed me for throwing her father out, and for her operation.[43]

Severe Neglect or Abuse

Some reasons for placement are easier to take and to understand than others. Abuse and neglect are often the hardest to deal with for both social workers and foster parents. We become angry when we think of a child being left alone, or without adequate food and clothing, or when a child is beaten and bruised. We cannot understand it and may judge these parents harshly without getting into their shoes. As we look at these parents it helps to say to ourselves, once they were children who were shaped and molded into what they are today. Studies indicate that often neglectful parents were unloved as children, and many abusive parents were abused as children.[44] Here are two stories of parents whose children were placed because of abuse or neglect.

> It was the coldest winter. Everyone was freezing to death. I was alone with the four kids. We had no heat and hot water. After the fire, we didn't have beds and most of our clothes were gone. So we just slept on the floor. I didn't care anymore, I knew the baby needed milk and warm clothes but what could I do? When the police came they sent me to the hospital, and took the kids away. I tried to fight them, but I had no strength left. I guess I knew they'd be better off without me. What could I do?

Another mother said:

> I couldn't stand the crying. She never stopped crying once since she was born. I was crying a lot myself since my husband left me when she was three months old. He used to beat me and I was glad he was gone. But I was scared alone. She was a colicky baby; cried all hours of the night. Nothing I could do would stop it. Finally I just hauled off and smacked her. She cried louder than ever. I grabbed her by the shoulders and shook her in the crib. I guess her head hit the headboard; she went limp. I thought she was dead. I was so scared. I rushed her to Emergency and told the doctor she fell off the bed. She had a mild concussion and was OK in a few days. I swore never to do it again. But the crying never stopped. I

continued to hit her when she cried. The second time I had to go to the hospital I jerked her arm so hard it came out of the socket. This time I told them what I did and they referred me to the social worker.

Sexual Abuse

Child sexual abuse has long been a problem in our society, but it has just recently become a topic for public discussion. Thinking and reading about child sexual abuse is likely to make you feel revulsion and disbelief. In a national study of all types of reported maltreatment, the American Humane Association reported that there has been an "increase in the percentage of sexual abuse cases from 3% in 1976 to 13% in 1984. About half of the sexual abuse perpetrators in the 1984 sample were natural parents and 32% were step, foster or adoptive parents."[45]

It may be extremely difficult to feel any compassion for parents and relatives who abuse children sexually. This kind of child abuse and neglect may be the true challenge of walking that extra mile!

Child sexual abuse is defined as exploiting dependent children "through such action as incest, molestation and rape."[46] Other important factors for consideration in child sexual abuse are the age and power difference between the child and abuser, the child's ability to understand the nature of the act, and the presence of force and coercion.

Females are more often sexually abused than males. The female victim is more likely to know the abuser, often a relative, while the male victim's abuser is more likely to be an acquaintance or stranger.[47]

Research findings suggest that adults who abuse children sexually have themselves experienced "early histories characterized by conflict, disruption, abandonment, abuse and exploitation."[48] No specific social or psychological factors can be identified as to the reason why an adult would be sexually interested in children. It is believed that this inappropriate behavior of sexually abusing children serves four needs or functions: "an outlet for sexual feelings; an expression of angry feelings; an effort to express and receive affection; and an opportunity to exert power."[49]

Although it is not possible to predict what factors contribute to sexual abuse in a cause-and-effect way, there are some family and environmental dynamics that may contribute. These factors may include:

A father or stepfather who is ineffectual, has low self-esteem, and is unable to relate adequately to other adults. He may be an autocratic ruler of the family.

An unhealthy marital relationship in which the adult sexual relationship is either strained or nonexistent.

Prolonged absence or loss of one parent

Severe overcrowding

Lack of social and emotional contacts outside the family

Geographical isolation

Alcoholism

Precipitating crisis in adult's life with a resulting loss of self-esteem

Cultural attitudes and multigenerational patterns of incest[50]

Here are two stories of parents and relatives whose children were placed because of sexual abuse. One father reported:

My wife was in the hospital and had been sick for a long time. Taking care of the apartment and the kids was really tough! Laura (14 years old) is a good kid and really helped out taking care of her younger brother, cooking and washing. She tried to make me feel better by bringing me the paper and a beer at night. I just didn't feel like she was my little girl any more, she looked and acted so grown up.

A retarded uncle's story:

Darlene's my niece and she's eight. We all lived together since she was a baby. I was 15 when she was born. She always liked me. I lost my job sweeping at the store. There's nothing to do. There's no one to talk to. I get bored watching TV all day. There usually isn't anyone at home when Darlene gets home from school and I'm so happy to see her. Sometimes I get real mad at her cause she doesn't want to play with me—she says I'm too old to play and I'm retarded. Boy does that make me mad! Darlene was real mad at me for touching her and said she was going to tell on me. I kept telling her I wasn't doing anything bad and no one would believe her anyway. When she wouldn't let me touch her, or said she was going to tell on me, I'd hit her hard and not be nice to her.

Family Problems

In a sense, all of the situations discussed so far were also family problems. If families are strong and supportive enough, placement is often avoidable. But when families come apart at their seams, both parents and children are in trouble. It is often hard to know what comes first, the chicken or the egg. When one or both parents desert the home, or become alcoholics, or addicted to other drugs, or when parents constantly fight, even physically, or are sexually abusive, placement of the children may be hard to avoid. It is not easy to understand how a parent becomes so self-absorbed, or literally absorbed in alcohol or drugs, or in constant brutal fighting, or exploiting a child. Desertion or abandonment is even harder to understand. But people have reasons for flight that they may never share or be consciously aware of. Seldom do we know the whole story.

Alcoholism and drug addiction are extremely high risk factors for parental abuse or neglect. Alcoholics have poor impulse control while inebriated and the battering of children and spouses is often related to drinking behavior. The later stages of alcoholism in which the alcoholic passes out, has DT's and serious memory problems, also precipitates neglect. Neglect is more common in drug abusers, who are unable to perform everyday tasks while high and may also become immobilized or unconscious.[51] In New York City, for example, placement in foster care from 1985–1987 spiked unexpectedly with the increased use of crack and cocaine as precipitating factors.[52]

With our ecological perspective, we know that the causes

of substance abuse are many and complex and that other factors combine with substance abuse to precipitate child maltreatment. According to all authorities on substance abuse, however, the parent who is a substance abuser must be treated for this condition before he or she can be engaged effectively in working on other difficulties.[53] Here are two stories of severe family problems leading to placement.

A father who was deserted says:

> ...[F]our weeks ago my wife ran away from home with another man. She left me, our home and children and went to Puerto Rico. I was desperate, being alone with the children and having no one to take care of them while I worked, so it was necessary to put them in homes until I could think more clearly. I didn't think my wife and I had any problems. We were happy until one day a month ago she asked if she could go to the movies. I said yes and she went out and never came back. Now looking back I remember that a few months ago she began to say she was bored and sick of everything...I just laughed it off. What an idiot I was. She was seeing another man.[54]

An aunt of a seven-year-old girl who went into placement said of her alcoholic sister, the child's mother:

> She drank to excess and had been living in rooming houses financed by welfare. The child was underfed and undernourished. We tried to help her and then washed our hands of it. She was no longer my sister as far as I was concerned. This Christmas I visited her and she was in bad shape with arthritis, lying on the floor and unable to move. The child took care of herself. We took the child and called the Board of Health. My sister was starving. The welfare doctor sent her to a hospital but they said they had no room for her. My pet peeve is why didn't the welfare worker do anything about it. When we told them she was an alcoholic they didn't believe it. Empty bottles were all over the apartment. The welfare center pleaded with us to keep [her] but it is not our problem....She was getting too attached to us. I called welfare and said I would leave the child at his desk....They said I

should take her to a hospital for a check-up. Finally she was placed [in a shelter].[55]

Adolescent Biological Parents

Adolescent parenthood is a problem of increasingly significant proportions and concern. The majority of adolescent parents keep their babies with the help of their families and social services. Some adolescent parents and/or their babies are placed in foster care. There is no evidence that adolescents maltreat their children more than other segments of society, but there is ample evidence that they and their children are at high risk for serious medical problems and for poverty related to incomplete education and unemployment due to child care responsibilities and low skill levels. Mother and infant mortality rates and low birth weights are highly associated with adolescent motherhood, because of the earlier age of childbearing and poor prenatal care. Adolescent mothers are likely to have more pregnancies than the average. Their children are likely to be raised in poverty, with a poor outlook for educational attainment and potentially serious long-term medical problems related to low birth weights and low Apgar scores.[56]

With resources and nurturing help from families, including foster families, adolescent parents can be helped to develop good parenting skills and to find ways to break the cycle of poverty. They need role models, as well as caregivers for their children, if they are to become self-sufficient and capable as parents. Foster parents can play a critically important part in making this happen. Preferably, adolescent parents in need of placement would be placed together with their children so that they can learn while mutual bonding and attachment proceed normally. Unfortunately, there are not enough mother-baby foster care programs where both can be placed together. There are none that we know of for teenage families, so that the young father can be helped to grow and assume responsibility for child care along with his partner. Our systems, inadequate at best, thereby perpetuate female heads of households and the lack of bonding of the young mother and child when they cannot be placed together.

Adolescent fathers have often not been taught parental responsibility despite their desire to take on the role. Adolescent mothers who place their children are often faced with expectations of maturity not easy to attain. Adolescent parents often face the loss of significant caregivers and of the child. They face fear and loneliness as they recognize the tasks of independent living and their own limitations and lack of resources and support. Many experience a further loss of self-esteem as they cannot manage meager finances and daily household demands as easily as they had envisioned. They may mask depression with anger and aloofness.[57] It is not easy to get beyond this facade and establish supportive relationships with adolescent parents, but it is essential if the teenagers are to care for themselves and eventually their baby on their own.

Knowing the reasons why teenagers have babies may help. Most teenage girls become pregnant unwittingly and unwillingly. Sexual activity among teenagers of all classes and racial/ethnic groups has become commonplace in the last 20 years. But most teenagers do not use contraception effectively enough to avoid pregnancy. They "take risks, engage in wishful thinking and are careless about preventing pregnancies."[58] Guilt and magical thinking accounts for some of the failure to use contraception.[60] Many girls feel that if "it just happens" they are not responsible for sexual intercourse and its consequences, as opposed to planning for contraception.[59] Beyond that, some teenagers (female and male) do not have adequate contraceptive information; some who have it fail to use it; and some believe having a baby is what the future holds as a way of becoming an adult.[60] Workers and foster parents can help teens to reach educational, vocational and group counseling resources that can enlighten them.[61] Foster parents can model good parenting with the children in their care, but also extend this caring to the teenage parent. Experiencing a caring parent teaches more than the best lecturers on parenting skills.

Foster parents can also avoid power struggles with teenage parents; can avoid taking an expert or "answer-person" role; can respect their right and need to find out for themselves; can avoid lecturing, and instead look for and praise the teenager's strengths.[62] By parenting the teenage parent, the foster parent can affect two, three, or more lives instead of just the infant they have in care. Here is a story of one teenage mother:

> I really love my daughter, Cherise, but it was a drag to have to take care of her all the time. I wanted to go out with my friends and party. School? Well, I liked it OK but I was absent and late a lot. The classes weren't very interesting. I wanted a job so I could earn some money to buy clothes and shoes. I dropped out of school. I thought I'd go out for a while because the party was just around the corner and Cherise was asleep. Mrs. Smith, upstairs, said she'd come down if Cherise cried. I only thought I'd be gone a while. I didn't know that I would stay away for two days. When I got back, the police had taken Cherise away. Now I cry all the time. I don't know what to do to get her back.

Here is a story of a 17-year-old mother.:

> I liked my foster mother, Mrs. Sands, but she wasn't like my real mother. My mama died two years ago. I really miss her and Sharon, we were a family. Mama would have really loved my baby Sharif, and I think she would have helped me take care of him. I left Mrs. Sands to live with Sharif's father, King, and his uncle. I thought King would care for us, he'd finished high school and was a security guard. We planned to get married when we saved enough money for the first month's rent and security. I love the baby, but all he does is eat, cry, and go to the bathroom. He's got a really bad rash. They told me it was from not changing his diapers often enough. I don't have the money to buy diapers, much less the medicine for the rash. King wants us to leave, he says the baby cries too much. My social worker says to place the baby or maybe she can find us a place together. I guess we'll live on the streets until then.

FOSTER PARENT FEELINGS ABOUT BIOLOGICAL PARENTS

Why is it so hard to relate to the biological parents sometimes?

As you have been reading, you have been thinking of the feelings you have about the various reasons for placement. Have you been angry at some of the parents? Have you felt sorry for some? Have you felt compassion for some? Foster parents have a right to know who the parents are, and why the child was placed. If the agency does not have any information, they need to know that too. Yet knowing has to be handled wisely, because feelings get communicated through what you don't say as well as through what you do say. This is also true for workers who may evade piercing questions from children about their parents. Somehow children know what you feel about their biological parents, and the parents know too. You need a chance to think this through for yourself so you can give helpful responses, by deed as well as word.

As Dr. Ner Littner recognizes, "It is not easy to be a foster parent. In many ways the pressures on foster parents are far greater than those encountered by parents looking after their own children. To the degree that foster parents are aware of these pressures, and to the degree that foster parents work at coping with these pressures, they make their tasks interesting, rewarding, and fulfilling. They will be able to accomplish their cherished goal of helping children who need their help."[63] Littner also recognizes that dealing with the biological parents is often the critical pressure or "trouble spot" for foster parents.[64] Evelyn Felker, a foster mother, says the same thing from the foster parent's shoes. "My inclination with some parents, unfortunately, is to forget they exist. Sometimes I want to think a beautiful child will not have to go back to a place where he was so unhappy. I have to fight that inclination, and so will you for the sake of yourself and the child."[65] Can you examine your thoughts and feelings as openly as Mrs. Felker did?

3

BIOLOGICAL PARENTS' FEELINGS

M uch has been said about maternal deprivation, or what it means for a child to be deprived of the parent. Have you ever thought about what it means to the parent to be deprived of the child— to be a mother without a child? Researchers have been finding that filial deprivation is an enormous loss to the parent. The feelings are the same whether the parent voluntarily placed the child or it was taken away by the court. Jenkins and Norman note that "almost all parents experienced some emotional reaction when children entered care. Sadness is the overriding feeling reported. But relief and thankfulness were also noted, as were guilt and shame, and these feelings tend to be situation oriented."[66] Anger was also a strong feeling, particularly in involuntary placements.

Let us look at the parents of Billy, Sally, Damien, Kim, and Mary. Perhaps their feelings had something to do with their behavior.

FEELINGS ABOUT PLACEMENT

Billy

I am Billy's mother, my name is Ruthie. I'm a very nervous person. I didn't mean for that water to fall on him. He was always under my feet; it just happened. I feel so guilty. I can't look him in the eyes again. I can't go to his foster home. What will they think of me? I can't sleep thinking about it myself.

I close my eyes and see Billy screaming. I'm so ashamed. I miss him so much. I need him. I wish it scalded me instead. I'm so nervous. I just can't face him again.

Sally

I'm Gloria, Sally's mother. I don't know why they didn't place her with her brothers. I feel more comfortable at their foster home, they're sort of outgoing and don't seem to mind my loud ways or my boyfriends. But at Gloria's foster home everything is proper. It scares me. The house is so nice and neat, they eat on time, they go to church. They must think I'm a sinner for sure. And Sally sitting by that window makes me feel so bad. What is she thinking? Her eyes condemn me. I can't take her home. I worry so much it makes me late. I take a little drink and bring a boyfriend along to give me courage. I want to give her something. She likes candy, but I wish I had money to buy her something real nice. Maybe I'd like to buy her a new mother and start all over again. I love my kids so much, how did it all go so wrong?

Damien

Yeah, so Damien was born with withdrawal symptoms, but that don't mean we're junkies. I mean we experimented a little bit, but they didn't have to take the kid. Well, Joe did mainline, but I never did. I could have taken care of him. They didn't even give me a chance. So what do I care? I can have more kids. Now they want us to sign for adoption. Forget it, we'll never sign especially to give him to those foster parents. They think they're so perfect, they don't even have good furniture. Oh what am I talking about? They're good people, but we don't have anything that counts, they have it all. I feel so empty inside. Why can't I leave Joe? Then they'd let me have him. Oh, forget it, I can't handle it anyway. I guess I'm just a junkie after all.

Kim

My name is Marian. I'm 15. I hate the way Mrs. Byrd looks at me when I visit Kim. She's just like my mother— she never says anything good and her looks could kill! I listen to my music because she leaves me alone with Kim and Kim is asleep. Then when Kim wakes up she looks at me and screams. I don't know what to do and put the music in her crib so she can hear it. But she just screams more. I heard enough screaming when my father beat my mother and brother. I can't take this anymore.

Mary

My husband Tom waits in the car. He has to go to AA therapy and probation before he can even see Mary again. He cries about it now and says he was too drunk to remember. But I don't believe him. How was I so dumb to believe him for so long? How was I blind for a year of my Mary's life? She's only 11 and what he did makes me sick. But I can't leave him now. He's gone through the detox and has been sober three months. He's irritable and still mean to me. He never hit me or Mary but he always yelled and threw things and still does! But now he also cries and tells me how sorry he is for all he's done. In marriage therapy he tells me he knows he was wrong and that he accepts now that he is an alcoholic. He says he loves us more than anything in the world. He's trying so hard now— how could I leave him? I'm a nervous wreck and need to talk with my social worker some more. It's so hard to go to these visits, especially when Mary asks about Tom.

FEELINGS ABOUT FOSTER PARENTS

What are these parents feeling? Are they feeling frightened, guilty, inadequate, inferior, angry, upset? How can you help?

Here are three parents who tell how they feel about foster parents who have been helpful to them. Do you see yourself in these examples?

Mrs. McAdams

The fact that you are visiting your child in a foster home is a reminder you are, at least for the time being, a failure as a parent. You are very sensitive, especially during the first visits. Sometimes a foster parent, in a well-meaning effort to let you know that your child is doing well in a foster home, will make comments on how well the child is eating, how neat he keeps himself and his room, how happy he is. To me, this type of remark was just an implied criticism of the care I had given my child, and was a verbal slap in the face.

It would have been easier to talk to my children if I had been kept up-to-date on what they had been doing. I understand that frequent phone calls can be very disruptive, but perhaps if a foster parent could just have dropped a brief note on a postcard once a week, it would have made communication between my child and me less strained.

It is surprising how many legitimate excuses you can come up with to avoid visiting your children in foster homes. Sometimes a failure to visit frequently on the part of the parents is not an indication that they don't care, but that they care too much.

You see your child in a home where everything seems orderly and calm, and quite often materially superior to anything you are going to be able to offer them, and you wonder why the hell you are bothering to rock the boat....sometimes staying away is the easiest for everyone, but when your whole life has been torn up and you are somehow trying to reassemble the pieces, I don't see how things could be easy.

The foster parent who gives you orders and instructions in the presence of your child is another problem. You are told that you should have the child back in the foster home at five o'clock, and admonished not to be late, or you are told to be sure little Tommy doesn't go outside without his sweater, because he has just recovered from a cold. These instructions may be necessary, but your kid, no matter how young, is already aware of the fact that you have little authority at this time, and this only increases the child's concern as to how responsible you are. If it is necessary to give the parent instructions about taking the child away from the foster home on an outing, it would be better to do so out of the child's presence.

No matter how courteous a foster parent is, the parents still have the feeling that they have very little to say in the decisions made for their child. There is no reason why the parents can't be consulted on some of the decisions about the child, even if they are only small ones, such as the color of a soon-to-be purchased coat or the advisability of getting a haircut. Being asked your opinion on matters concerning your child is a step toward the time when you will be making decisions yourself again, and will help restore your confidence in your ability to do so. I think it is the responsibility of both the social worker and the child's foster parent to involve the parent even if she doesn't show too much interest in being involved.[67]

Another Mother's Story

You're going to visit your children in somebody else's home. They are doing what you should be able to do for them. The guilt complex is overwhelming. You just can't describe it—walking into a house and having your children call somebody else Mommy and Daddy. You want them to. You want them to be treated as their own children. You want them to call them Mommy and Daddy, to feel this much relaxed with them, to go to them with their problems, but you don't want it. You are their mother. They are nothing but caretakers for the children, and this is very difficult to face. But I walked in the house anyway; I walked in the first foster parents' house that I walked into and was...Bless this woman, bless Lucille. I knocked on the door and the kids opened the door because they were expecting me and they went, "Mommy, Mommy," and they jumped all around me and I stood there stiffly afraid to walk in the front door.

She was in the kitchen...She said, "Hi, come right in. The coffee's on the stove, the cups are up here—grab a cup. Sit down and we'll talk." Like I was a neighbor, not like I was company coming to visit her home. Like I was a neighbor, this was something I did every day, I walked in and grabbed a coffee cup off the shelf, poured myself a cup and it totally relaxed me.

I think it might have scared me away if they had been dressed up for a Sunday afternoon visit, ushered me into the parlor where I sat there very stiffly and said to my children, "How do you do?" But here I was taken as a friend. I was not asked questions, not even, "How are you doing?" We talked about the weather and I don't really remember vividly, but I remember the conversations were very general....It was like two neighbors sitting down and talking.

She suggested to the children that they bring me outside to show me some pets that they had in the backyard, to give me a chance to be with my children without her making some excuse..."Well, I'll go upstairs and powder the nose." Bless this woman, Lucille.[68]

An Adolescent Parent's Story

Well, here I am in Mrs. Sands' foster home again. I couldn't make it on my own with Sharif. To get welfare I had to have an address but I couldn't get the rent money so I've got nothing. My boyfriend, King, put me out and went South, and—well, forget him! My friends too—some friends! But when my social worker called Mrs. Sands, she said she'd take me back. I was surprised. I wasn't very nice to her. She even said she'd take Sharif too. But my social worker had to get special permission for that so he had to go into temporary foster care. Some temporary! It took three months but then me and Sharif got to live together at Mrs. Sands'.

I really respect her. She went out of her way for me to take me back. She fixed up her room for us to be together and she moved into the small room. She even let me use her TV in my room. There are house rules and sometimes I still mess up— especially about not staying overnight. But I'm trying really hard.

Mrs. Sands don't take no stuff from me, but she's the first fair person I ever met. Well, maybe the second. Mrs. Berg, my social worker is OK too. She doesn't lecture me about King and got me Mrs. Sands back. Aunt Dotty, (that's what I call Mrs. Sands now) l-o-v-e-s Sharif. She cuddles him a lot. You know, I felt funny holding him but I tried to do like her and she said I was getting the hang of it real good. And she showed me how to take care of his rash and make his food. I'm back in the 10th grade. She doesn't let me go out after school until I stay with him a while. At first I didn't like it. I didn't know what to do with him. But she showed me how to play with him and when I saw him giggle so much I liked it too. Sometimes I wish I was the baby and she was my grandmother. She'll never take the place of my real mother, but she doesn't try to either. She says she loves me just like she loves Sharif. Sometimes I almost believe her.

You have now heard from three parents on the subject of foster parents. What would you say was most helpful in each situation? What do these parents see as the qualities of good foster parents or social workers?

4

CHILDREN'S FEELINGS AND CONNECTIONS

Why do I have to help the parents, why can't I just help the child? The child is a part of a family system just as you are. Family experts say the family is a system of interaction. There is no such thing as individual problems— all actions and interactions are part of a family process. A system is two or more units relating to each other in such a way that if there is a change in one it affects the other and the reaction of the second in turn affects the first.

Think of your own family. Can one hurt without the others hurting, or have a joyful moment without sharing it? Would a change in employment affect all of you? Or if one of the children became ill, wouldn't you all respond? If children go away to college or into the armed services, aren't they still a part of the family?

Foster children were also born into a family system; their removal from it throws it out of kilter. Part of our job is to restore that system— to help it reach a new and better balance with the child as a part of it.

CHILDREN AND THE FAMILY SYSTEM

When we think of children, we think of their parents, grandparents, aunts, uncles, cousins, and close family friends. A child's social network may also include neighbors, teachers, friends, shopkeepers, religious leaders, recreational leaders, and others. A social network is made up of "a person's subjective community, that is, those individuals, groups, and parts of formal organizations which have meaning, actually or potentially for a person."[69] The importance of the social network is recognized when we try to place children in their own communities. In that way the child does not suffer multiple losses at placement. We can help children in placement by strengthening and maintaining their ties in the social network. If possible, before placement we would also look to the network to mobilize helpers to prevent placement, but in any case, the social network for children and parents both before and after placement can be a source of strength and support. Often we mistakenly assume that people have no support network when there is no nuclear or close family available. In this way we may overlook a great deal!

A foster family becomes a support system for the child and family when these natural supports are overtaxed and temporarily unavailable. If we can see children in all of their connections, we can help them to maintain a sense of connectedness and to stay a part of it even though temporarily it cannot take them in.

A tool you can use to help the child and parent look at their social networks is called an eco-map, or ecological map. This paper and pencil tool was developed by Ann Hartman to help workers in public child welfare agencies examine the needs of families.[70] The map pictures the family or individual in its everyday life. Workers may use this map for assessment and intervention purposes.

In consultation with the worker, foster parents can also use the eco-map with children in their care and, when it seems that the parents would be comfortable, with the parents and children together.

The Eco-Map

The eco-map is a drawing of the ecological system, whose boundaries encompass the major systems that are a part of the family's life and the nature of the family's relationship with the various systems. It portrays an overview of the family— the important nurturant or conflict-laden connections between the family and the world. It shows the flow of resources and deprivations. It highlights points that touch and the conflicts to be mediated, the bridges to be built, and the resources to be sought and used. It saves time to have empty maps available. These maps can be worked on by an

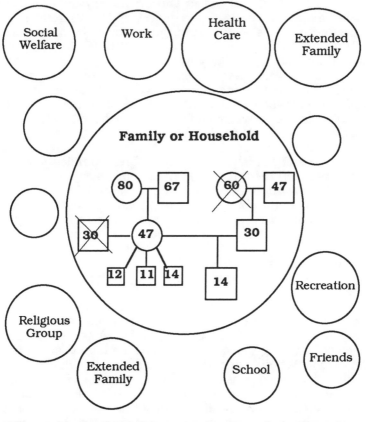

Fill in connections where they exist. Indicate nature of connections with a descriptive word or by drawing different kinds of lines: _____ for strong, -------------------- for tenuous, _\|\|\|\|\|_ for stressful. Draw arrows along lines to indicate flow of energy, resources, etc. _▸_▸_▸_▸_ Identify significant people and fill in circles as needed.

Figure 1. Eco-Map

individual or a family. Hartman gives the following directions in making the map:

Constructing an Eco-Map. First the nuclear family system or household is drawn in a large circle at the map's center (see figure 1). It has been common practice in mapping families to use squares to depict males and circles to depict females. Relationships are indicated as in the traditional family tree or genetic chart. It is useful to put the person's age in the center of the circle or square. Thus, a circle with "80" in the center would represent an elderly woman.

After drawing the household in the large circle in the middle, add the connections between the family and the different parts of the environment. Some of the most common systems in the lives of most families have been labeled, such as work, extended family, recreation, health care, school, and so on. Other circles have been left undesignated so that the map can be individualized for different families. Connections between the family and the various systems are indicated by drawing lines between the family and those systems. The nature of the connection can be expressed in the type of line drawn: a solid or thick line represents an important or strong connection, and a dotted line a tenuous connection; jagged marks across the line represent a stressful or conflicted relationship. It is useful to indicate the direction of the flow of resources, energy, or interest by drawing arrows along the connecting lines.

In testing the eco-map, it has been found that the use of the three kinds of lines for conflicted, strong, and tenuous relationships is an efficient shorthand when the worker uses the eco-mapping procedure, without the family, as an analytic tool. When using the map as an interviewing tool, however, this code has often been felt to be too constraining. Workers have preferred to ask clients to describe the nature of the connection and will then describe that connection by writing a brief description along the connecting line. Connections can be drawn to the family as a whole if they are intended to portray the total family's relationship with some system in the environment. Other connections can be drawn between a particular individual in the family and an outside system when that person is the only one involved, or different family members are involved with an outside system in different ways. This enables the map to highlight the contrasts in the way various family members are connected to the world. It is easy to learn to plot the eco-map and it is important to become comfortable with it before using it with clients. A simple way to learn is to sketch out one's own eco-map. It is also useful to practice with friends. By then, one is generally ready to use it with clients.[71]

Uses of the Eco-Map. No matter how the eco-map is used, its main value is in its visual impact and its ability to organize and present not only a great deal of factual information but also the relationships between variables in a situation. The connections, the themes, and the quality of the family's life seem to jump off the page. The visual experience has great integrative value for the client.

At first the eco-map was used to organize a whole picture and to make an assessment of supports and stressors in the environment. Before long, though, it became apparent that the eco-map would be useful in interviewing. Client and worker cooperated in picturing the client's life space. This led to a collaborative worker-client relationship and much more active participation on the part of the client in the information-gathering and assessment process. According to Hartman, "The eco-map has been extensively tested with parents working toward the return of their placed children through the Temporary Foster Care Project of the Michigan Department of Social Services. Foster care workers noted that parents who were generally angry and self-protective following placement of their children because of abuse or neglect were almost without exception engaged through the use of the map. Workers were aware of a dramatic decrease in defensiveness. The ecological perspective made it clear to parents that the worker was not searching for their inner defects but rather was interested in finding out what it was like to be in the clients' space, to walk in their shoes."[72]

PRESERVING ETHNIC AND RELIGIOUS IDENTIFICATIONS

We have said that children are a part of a nuclear family, an extended family, and a community with social networks. These are, for the most part, tangible things. But children are also a part of other less tangible systems, like their religious or ethnic group. Ties to both should be maintained because they are a source of feeling connected, and of individual and familial identity. Efforts to place children within their religious groups are usually made except for highly exceptional circumstances. Children are also usually placed within their racial groups, but ethnicity itself is not attended to well enough when considering placements.

Monica McGoldrick, John Pearce. and Joseph Giordano, in their now classic work, *Ethnicity and Family Therapy*,[73] define the ethnic group as "those who conceive of themselves as alike by virtue of their common ancestry, real or fictitious, and who are also so regarded by others....[It] describes a sense of commonality transmitted over generations....It is more than race, religion, or national and geographic origin (which is not to minimize the significance of race or the special problems of racism). It involves conscious and unconscious processes that fulfill a deep psychological need for identity and historical continuity....It plays a major role in determining what we eat, how we work, how we relax, how we celebrate holidays and rituals, and how we feel about life and death and illness."[74]

We know that identity, continuity, and belonging are central issues in the lives of foster children. Helping children to learn about their ethnic group can strengthen their family ties, their sense of identity and continuity, and their self-esteem. Ignoring a child's ethnic difference, far from showing tolerance, may well inadvertently give out the negative message that the child's ethnic group is not as good as the foster family's ethnic group.

When foster families share the same ethnic ties as the children and their families, it may be helpful to share special rituals and holidays. When children and their families have different roots than the foster families, it may be helpful to involve the biological family in bringing ethnic food for a celebration, or in sharing in preparing for holidays or rituals. You may help the child to find music and reading on her or his ethnic group, and involve the parent in teaching the child and foster family about the culture. You may accompany the parent and child to ethnic celebrations in the community as their guest. You will find creative ways to help children celebrate their ethnicity, which can help in bridging the differences between the families and affirming the child's identity. Of course, it would also be nice to have the parent, along with the child, celebrate some of your ethnic holidays as well!

Language is an important part of ethnic identity. To

preserve language is to preserve identity. Where children's families speak another language it would help to encourage the children to preserve their language. Perhaps they can teach it to the foster family as well. Children need to know that their language heritage is valued, and their families need to know it as well. The book by McGoldrick and her colleagues has chapters on 22 different ethnic groups popularly found in the United States. They also supply references for many others. The chapters on Italian, Irish, Jewish, Asian, Native American, Afro-American, West Indian, and Puerto Rican families may be particularly helpful in today's placement scene.[75] It would help if the worker and foster family could use these resources to understand and appreciate the ethnic heritage of the foster child, whatever that heritage may be.

DEALING WITH DIFFERENCE

We have just spoken about dealing with ethnic differences, but there are many other differences that foster parents and workers will encounter in working with foster children and their families. For example, the parent may be a physically or mentally challenged person with disabilities, or the parent may be gay. We should examine each of these differences, and what our thoughts and feelings may be in encountering a situation of difference.

Parents with Disabilities

In the old days we used to see people who had differences in hearing, vision, mobility, mental abilities or other aspects of physical and mental functioning as "the disabled." An outgrowth of the Disability Rights Movement, however, has in recent years been a redefinition of terms. The words "the disabled" emphasizes what a person cannot do and has negative connotations.[76] New concepts replacing those negative words are to be physically or mentally challenged or to be persons with disabilities, that is, to be people who face ongoing exceptional tasks in living due to a limitation in physical or mental functioning. These tasks are seen as challenges, not as handicaps. For example, those with severe hearing, visual, or mobility challenges may still live a full and rewarding life as they develop the skills to cope with, and adapt to, their particular difference. These days there are centers for independent living that help people acquire coping skills, including living alone or in group situations in the community for those who are wheelchair-bound, paraplegic or quadraplegic; those who are blind or deaf. If the conditions have existed since birth or childhood, the challenges to coping may have been met early on and no additional help may be needed in adulthood. If the onset of the condition occurred in later life, as for those in a traumatic accident or with chronic diseases with later onset (like diabetes or multiple sclerosis, for example), some degree of help in learning to cope with the new challenge may be needed. A child in your care may have a parent who is chronically physically challenged. Your positive view of this parent can be very helpful to the child.

We must struggle with the myths that people with such challenges are dependent, immature, unable to cope, and in need of constant protection. We must make accurate appraisals of strengths and abilities and see people as individuals first and individuals with disabilities, second.

According to Haraguchi, people with disabilities often struggle with lowered self-esteem because they are thwarted in efforts toward independence.[77] In some cases they must be more dependent than they would like, and in some cases, well-meaning others may naturally tend toward an unhelpful level of overprotection.[78]

Even though the vast majority of people with disabilities have children who are not physically or mentally challenged, the myth of producing "damaged children," or being unable to cope with child rearing persists.

One foster family found it difficult when a wheelchair-bound father whose very thick eyeglasses gave him an odd appearance, visited his children in the foster home. Until they got to know the father, they harbored many stereotypes about him. His children were delighted to see him, but the foster parents' children seemed frightened of him, and the foster parents found it difficult at first to reach out to him. The worker helped the father and the foster parents to communicate. The father grew comfortable enough to indulge his story-telling abilities with the foster family. As everyone laughed or cried with his wonderful renditions of popular children's stories, the atmosphere relaxed and visiting became an occasion everyone cherished.

Another foster family was helpful to a depressed, newly blind mother. Their faith in her abilities and the warmth and acceptance extended during the visiting helped her find her confidence in rearing her children once again. After the children returned home, the foster family continued as a strong support system.

Parents or Children with AIDS

The AIDS crisis has necessitated the placement of children with AIDS and of children who do not have the disease but whose parents do and hence, the visiting of biological parents who have AIDS. Since AIDS has been surrounded by unusual fear and mythology, it is important to state the facts so people can deal with fears, myths, and feelings.

> AIDS is a devastating disorder of the immune system, (caused by a virus called HIV). It impairs the body's natural immunity, taking away the ability to fight infection, and leaving the person with AIDS susceptible to serious diseases that are little threat to any person with a normal immune system....There are only a few known ways to get AIDS: through sexual intercourse; through an exchange of blood via shared contaminated needles or drug paraphernalia; or through the exchange of contaminated blood or blood products, including transmission from infected mother to developing fetus or from the nursing mother to the infant....Children who are sexually abused are also at risk.

> There are ways AIDS is *not* transmitted. We can't get it through casual contact. We can't get it by talking to someone, by shaking hands, hugging, coughing or sneezing, from sitting on a toilet, from spending time with people with AIDS, or from going to the same school. We can't get it by giving blood. AIDS is not a "gay disease." While the first major outbreak in this country was in the male homosexual population, in several countries heterosexuals are the most com-

monly afflicted. The incidence among heterosexuals in this country is rising. They may be subjected to the cruelest forms of discrimination. They may be plunged into poverty by the expense of medical treatment or loss of their job, or both. Their children may be shunned. Their family, friends, or colleagues may reject them. They must face disability and certain death.[79]

Yet the tendency to pass moral judgments may interfere with our empathy for parents with AIDS.

The chain of infection in AIDS may pull mothers and their children down together. It is projected that the number of children under 13 showing symptoms of the AIDS infection will reach 10,000— and could climb to 20,000 by 1991.[80] Their mothers and fathers are also often afflicted. Families will do what they must and what they can, and foster care will also be increasingly necessary. *Newsweek* recently carried a powerfully moving story of a grandmother who after mourning the loss of her daughter to AIDS resumed the care of her three grandchildren, two of whom also had AIDS, as did her son-in-law.[81] Can you imagine her anguish? If she had been unable to care for the children, they might well have been placed in foster care. Does the information that you cannot catch AIDS casually help you reach out with love and caring to parents with AIDS?

George Getzel and Diego Lopez in their article, "Strategies for Volunteers Caring for Persons with AIDS," stress that "every person with AIDS is innocent. The AIDS virus does not inventory the virtues or sins of potential victims....No person chooses to get AIDS. Blame is cast by human beings who for selfish reasons lay their curses upon persons in acute distress with AIDS."[82] If you, too, can withhold judgment— if you can walk a mile in their shoes— you will be able to extend much-needed support and acceptance to families and children facing illness and death under a cloud of stigma. According to Getzel, "The inclusion of a person with AIDS in family life cycle events like baptisms, weddings, bar mitzvahs and holiday rituals breaks down social isolation and allows for opportunities to participate in meaningful occasions that represent continuity and contribution."[83] How do you feel about making a contribution to your fellow human beings at this time of greatest need? How would you reach out to a parent with AIDS?

The Chronically Mentally Challenged

Mental health, mental capacities, and physical health are interrelated parts of the whole human being. In reality we can not separate the mind and body. We have noted earlier that what has been called mental illness is now known not to be purely emotional, psychological or even psychosocial, but has biochemical, organic, and genetic bases. To blame people for their own brain disease is to infer a control over often mysterious biological factors at work.[84] Similarly, while the exact causation of most mental retardation and other developmental disabilities is unclear (other than certain genetic syndromes) we do know that they also have some biological base.[85] People with any form of mental illness or mental retardation (or other specific learning disabilities) are chronically mentally challenged. They face the exceptional tasks of coping with daily life and stressful situations: for the mentally ill, distinct problems in thought and feeling; and in thought and learning for the mentally retarded. Yet it is clear that the chronically mentally challenged can often function as parents and as individuals. This sometimes takes continual support and learning. Though mental illness and mental slowness are two distinct and usually unrelated entities, they have a common thread in that acceptance, a caring support network, and education for living can help them a great deal.[86]

Mild mental illness or mental retardation may be unnoticeable to the untrained eye and we may expect far too much of biological parents with such conditions. Any mental challenge presents major tasks in adapting to and coping with life. By genuinely accepting differences and by teaching compensatory skills, we can enhance the parenting abilities that can reunify families.

People with more serious levels of mental difficulties may look different to us. Psychotropic medication for those with mental illness may take its toll in their gait and spontaneity, and their level of activity and appearance, even though intelligence may be average or above. While the mildly retarded (I.Q. 50 to 70) or moderately retarded (I.Q. 35 to 50) individual is not usually taking psychotropic medication, they too may look odd or different. They may speak slowly or with difficulty, may have the physical signs of Downs Syndrome, or may not seem dressed appropriately. They may not be thinking at an age-appropriate level. But they are working hard at learning and coping. The acceptance and gentle role-modeling of the foster parent and worker, and the teaching extended to mentally challenged parents can raise self esteem and promote competence and mastery in the parents and also in foster children who desperately need to feel that their parents are "as good as anybody's!"

Gay or Lesbian Biological Parents

"It is estimated that a minimum of 10 percent of the population are homosexually oriented. Lesbians and gays are members of every race, religion, socioeconomic, and ethnic groups in American society....There are as many gay lifestyles as there are gays."[87] Gay people may therefore also be parents of children in care. This may not be obvious to workers and foster parents because many people hide being gay. Yet, many more have discovered that to be a full human being their sexual orientation must become part of their identity in private and open ways. Far from feeling negative about their identity, gay people feel a sense of wholeness, integrity, and pride about themselves as gays. The parent who feels comfortable with gayness may bring it to the awareness of the worker and the foster parent. Most likely in that case, the children are already aware of the parent's identity. It may also be shared as a source of struggle, for even when gay people feel good about themselves, they know that they have to struggle continually against the biases, myths, and sometimes violent reactions of other members of society. One lesbian mother told the worker about her identity and her struggles with discrimination, once the plan for returning the children home was well under way. She confided that she was afraid to tell about this before the worker showed confidence in her child-rearing abilities. As a recovering alcoholic, now sober for three years, she feared another stigmatized label and its effects. The children were relieved when the worker knew, because they had been uncomfortable about hiding this from the worker. They too had feared that the knowledge would prevent their return home, which they wanted more than anything.

Biological parents already face stigma as parents who had to give up children. They also may hesitate to reveal their being gay, because the legal system has been biased against gay parents to the point of the loss of child custody in about 50% of the cases to the nongay parent or to the courts.[88] Indeed, workers would have to be very careful about the confidential nature of such a disclosure should they be entrusted with it. Moreover, workers and foster parents can be helpful to gay parents who have been able to tell their children about being gay by showing their acceptance to both parent and child. It is very important, therefore, for foster parents and workers to examine their own feelings and the myths they hold about this sexual minority group.[89]

It will help to use positive words as well as to convey your understanding and acceptance of this difference. The word gay is more acceptable within the gay community than the word homosexual. Terms like dyke, faggot, queer…are equivalent to hate terms and epithets used against racial and ethnic minorities."[90]

"Of the estimated 20 million gay persons in this country, probably at least one-third of the lesbian and around 10% of the gay males have children, though not all have custody."[91] The following are some misconceptions and myths about gay parents:

Gay parents will raise gay children. There is absolutely no evidence to support this belief. The vast majority of lesbians and gay men are raised by heterosexual parents.

Proselytizing. Another worry nongays have is that gay parents will try to convince their children to be gay. Although there is no evidence that gay parents do try to persuade their children to be gay, and some evidence to the contrary, it is unlikely that efforts at persuasion in either direction would have much effect.

Gay parents and their children's gender role development. At present there is some evidence that children of gay parents show no difference in gender role behavior from children of nongay parents.

Children of gays will be damaged by growing up in deviant homes. There is no evidence that children suffer disproportionately because of their parent's sexual preference. Lewis found in her study that the children expressed more difficulty with their parent's divorce than with their mother's lesbianism....The children were proud of their mother for challenging society's rules and standing up for what she believed....The parent's sexual preference does not matter as much as the love, caring and maturity of the adults and their effort to help the children become self-reliant and self-assured."[92]

It is also a myth that gays are "child molesters." With regard to this belief, Riddle states that "97 percent of child molesters are heterosexual males."[93]

We have asked you to consider biological parents with many types of differences— ethnic and race differences, physical and mental challenges, and stigmatized statuses, including having AIDS or being gay. It is likely that you will encounter parents who have some of these differences. It is hoped that you have used your mind and heart to walk another extra mile to take in knowledge and to find compassion for difference in your fellow human beings. No foster parent or worker can be without this. People are, above all, individuals. When you are able to respect difference and individualize all people, you are ready to provide care for children and be supportive to families. Children in foster care long to remain connected to their own families and to view them positively. When our families are viewed positively, we have positive self esteem.

SEPARATION

From birth to death we experience many separations. In childhood, they are part of becoming self-reliant adults. Somehow, they are never easy, and the way we deal with them in early years may influence our later handling. From our initial separation at birth to letting go of mother's hand and walking alone, or our first day at school, we build upon experiences of separation as growth producing, if a little scary. As we are reassured that our families will still be there for us when we return, we are able to venture forth.

Foster children are often taken away from mothers and fathers with no real reassurance of their return, for indeed the parents are suddenly no longer there. As Dr. Littner says:

The placed child never really understands why his natural parents have left him. No matter what the realistic reason for the placement, the placed child develops a series of irrational explanations that he buries deeply in his mind...he was placed because he was bad and the placement is his punishment; his natural parents have rejected and abandoned him and he will never see them again; his natural parents have lied; etc. etc. A child may need help expressing his feelings for they are often in conflict. He may both love and hate the parents who left him. He may feel that placement "is being done to him" and he cannot control his situation. We must remember that no child wants his parents more than a rejected child.[94]

Do you think a child should talk about those feelings? Eight-year-old Travis thought so:

The social worker asked Travis how he felt about leaving home. Travis was very quiet, pensive. The worker tried again— how did it make you feel? Travis answered: "I felt dull." The social worker asked what does one do when one feels dull? Travis answered, "Just sits down." The social worker asked, "Just sit down and wait for it to go away?" Travis said "um." The social worker asked, "Does anything help to make it go away faster?" Travis said only one thing. The social worker asked, "What's that?" Travis replied, "When somebody talks to me." [95]

THE HIDDEN PARENT

Consider the following: "The absent parent becomes an important part of a child's 'fantasy life' and has strong directional influence on what a child will become and how comfortably he can live with himself. When social workers and foster parents ignore the absent parent, it is to the child as though they had killed her. Parents artificially killed in this way will 'arise from the dead' and haunt!"[96]

Although we may prefer to feel that out of sight is out of mind, it really isn't so for the foster child. Your attention is needed to help the child think about what has happened to himself or herself and to his or her parents. According to Almeda Jolowicz, who wrote an important article entitled *The Hidden Parent*, "We have to accept the concept that the child does have an inner life in which he maintains a parent-child relationship. There are numberless cases to prove that the physical separation of parent and child is not a sufficient measure to interrupt the influence of the biological parent upon the child. On the contrary, the separation may lead to the child's *idealizing* the parent."[97]

Lila illustrates this. Lila came to the Halls when she was seven. She immediately began a pattern of sitting alone in her room. When other children were playing outside, she would quietly slip up to her room. When the Halls asked what she was doing in her room, she answered,"Thinking." When they asked her finally what she thought of while sitting alone in her room, she replied: "I think about my daddy. I miss him. I think he has a beautiful house for me somewhere. But I don't know where." She then opened her thoughts to them, and the foster parents were astonished at all the work Lila was doing in piecing her life together.

The following is an excerpt from a group discussion of teenage foster girls and the social worker in the agency. The longing for their parents and the idealizing of them is readily apparent as the girls try to help each other with these painful feelings.

> Cherise said sadly that she doesn't think that anyone loves you like your natural mother who "birthed" you. The others agreed. Pat said, "Once mine bought me a fur coat, I know she's rich wherever she is." Cherise said, "I heard my father has a yacht in Coney Island." Maya asked if Cherise ever went on the yacht? Cherise admitted she had never even seen her father. Maya said that her mother left her when she was a baby, but she knew she was still coming back. She was sick and lost the address where Maya is— but she'd find it. Pat said angrily, "Social workers can't do anything for us except bring our mothers back." Every eye turned to the worker. After a silence the worker responded, "No one can bring a mother or father back and I can hear you are all angry about that. You are also wondering about what life would

have been like with your parents, you hope it would be better than what you have now." Nods and comments in strong agreement. The worker said, "It is rough, but perhaps this group can help to make things better for you by helping you to deal with the things on your mind and the way things are now." We shared a thoughtful, close silence, and they began to clean up our meeting room. [98]

Foster children need to be encouraged to express their thoughts, feelings, and fantasies about their parents and how and why they were placed.

Evelyn Felker, a foster parent, gives some helpful hints on this subject.

Because the child does not remember the parent or does not talk about the absent parent, does not relieve you of the responsibility to keep communication open. Of course, you do not want to stir up emotional debris of a settled situation. But in most cases you can make a casual reference, such as, "You must have gotten those pretty blue eyes from your mother," or "Did you know your daddy was over six feet tall?" For the child who may want to ask questions and is afraid you do not want him [sic] to, this is sufficient opening. [99]

TOOLS TO HELP CHILDREN

The Family Tree

It is very popular today for families to trace their roots. Have you ever wondered who your ancestors are and where they came from? If the worker thinks it is a good idea, foster parents might like to develop this family tree for themselves and the foster child. It is a fascinating activity to do together, because it is fun and it shows the foster parents' willingness to let the child have two families.

With the parent's permission, you will need to dig up the foster child's family history (see figure 2). Remember most of us don't know who all or even most of our ancestors are.

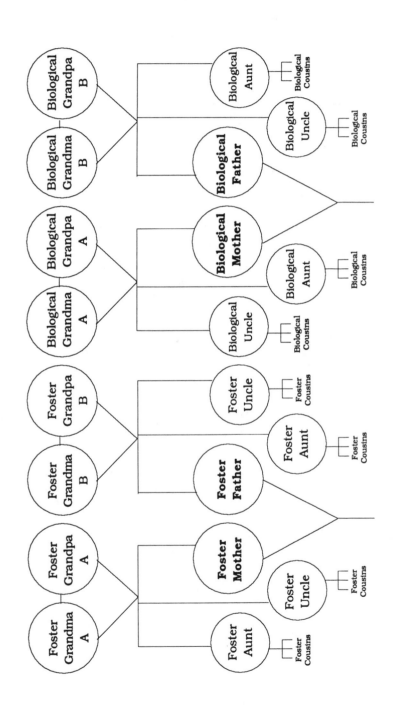

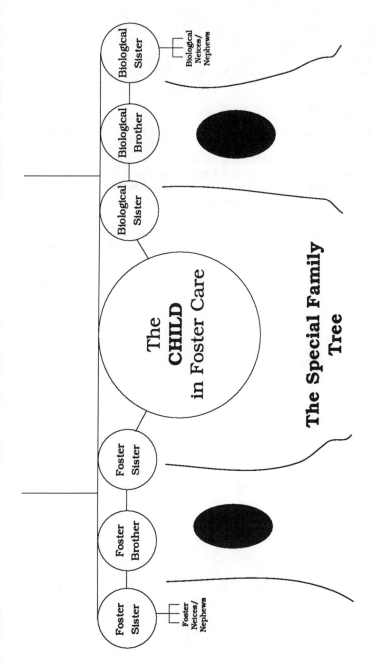

Figure 2. The Family Tree

Members of the biological family would be the best informants and it would also involve them nicely with the child. Placing the foster parents' family tree next to the child's tree shows by the connection that the foster child is a part of two families. The questions this may raise for the child will be important ones that deserve discussion and honest, understanding answers according to the age of the child.

The Life Book

Another thing to do is to make a "Story-of-My-Life Album" with the child. Worker's may do the Life Book with the children alone or involve the foster parents and the biological parents. Foster parents may also guide the effort when the worker thinks this is a good idea in a given situation. You can involve the parents in bringing pictures and memorabilia and in working on the album with the child. It should include a copy of the child's birth certificate, baptismal papers, and all available records and pictures and important "quotes" of family members including names of all the people the child has lived with from birth to the present. It can reflect the child's life with the biological family and the foster family. The trees and the album are a way of helping foster children to pull their lives together.

5

YOUR HELPING ROLE

As you have considered the preceding case situations you may have felt "there are so many problems— how can I help—where do I pitch in?" When you add up how important the parents are to the children, the importance of your helping the parents becomes clear. Essentially, you provide them with a role model for dealing with the environment, for caring, and for mothering, and for family life.[100] Some biological parents have never had good enough mothering or much of a family life. As Charnley says, "The love-starved parents are as entitled to compassion as are the love-starved children."[101] This implies that you can provide a nurturing relationship for the parent. You can also become part of the parent's support system, whose weakening or breakdown was partly responsible for the placement. You can become a strong new support link.

ROLE MODELING

Although social workers and foster parents both provide support and help to the biological parents, foster parents are in the best position to model parenting. The child is a part of the foster family, which is now the child's frame of reference for family life. Role-modeling takes place by word and deed. You might be able to tell the parent how you operate, but more will be "caught than taught." As you provide a relaxed and friendly atmosphere for visiting in your home, the modeling will go on: loving and caring; sharing and giving; structure and limits; discipline; solving daily problems; mutual respect; individual separation and growth; patience, tolerance of difference, and fair play; dealing with painful and positive feelings; communication; household management and child management techniques.[102] Foster families will also be modeling a nurturing environment; strong parenting skills; knowledge of community resources; and relationship skills.[103]

NURTURING

You provide an atmosphere of warmth, understanding, caring, and structure for foster children. You accept children for what they are, even though you may not accept some of their behavior. This is called nurturing. You may also extend nurturing to the parents. Each one of us provides love and caring in our own way. Some of us are outgoing and demonstrative; others are more quietly respectful and accepting. You must stay with your own style of expression with both foster children and the parents. As we have seen, the parents are usually very hard on themselves, full of guilt and self-recrimination. Your acceptance and respect can be a strong force in building the self-esteem and competence they must have if they are ever to take their children home.

PROVIDING A SUPPORT SYSTEM

Studies have shown that people rely on natural helping networks. They may or may not be bound by geography or distance, but are made up of reliable and dependable relationships, such as a neighbor who brings a pot of soup to a sick neighbor, or another neighbor who is willing to mind the children when needed, or a friend who provides a shoulder to cry on when one faces a great loss.[104] Can you be such a person in the network of the biological parents?

EVELYN FELKER'S PRINCIPLES FOR FOSTER PARENTS

Support the Parents' Efforts To Parent

By your standards a particular mother may be inadequate and it may seem as though she only makes things worse for the child when she acts. But you have to start somewhere. Let me give an example. The parent asks as she brings the child home to you after a visit, "Does Sue need anything I could get her?" So you think a minute and say, "Well, yes. She could use a dress to wear when the choir at school gives its concert next month. It's supposed to be fairly simple and a pastel color. She takes a size 10 now." Next week the parent brings the dress. It is red-dotted swiss, with seven ruffles of black down the skirt, white collar and cuffs, and is marked "dry clean only."

Your first reaction may be to treat the parent like a not-too-bright teenager. You use the occasion to impress on the parent just how inadequate she is. You say that the dress will not do because it is the wrong color—you told her pastel. You ask her to take it back and get some underwear. (You probably will not get the underwear and I do not blame the mother.) Then you point out to Sue that she does not have a new dress for the concert like the other girls because her mother did not get the right one, even though you told her what Sue needed.

Something like the following is what you should say. You thank her for the dress, let Sue try it on so the mother can see how pretty it looks, and mention that though you are not sure they are going to wear any red dresses to the concert, there is another occasion coming up when the dress will be just right. You explain to Sue that this is a very good dress and she will be able to wear it only for special occasions because it must be dry-cleaned. But then it's too pretty to wear just any old time, anyway. You can comment that the size 10 fits and it is lucky her mother was able to judge her size so well.

Do you think the first reaction was extreme and that anyone would know better than to react that way? Not at all....Be honest about your own feelings. You will find that the reaction is natural, and must be fought. The principle of accepting what the parent can do now in a way that encourages better performance in the future needs constant, imaginative application.

Play Second Fiddle to the Parents

The next principle calls for unselfishness. If you are doing a proper job of parenting a foster child, the great bulk of his needs is being met by you. But he has one need you cannot meet— he needs to be able to love his parents. This works out differently at different ages, but the need is never absent. You hope his need is met eventually by a corresponding need of his parents to love him, and you do all you can to foster and strengthen love between them.

No matter how long he lives with you, you must be willing to accept the fact that the child has membership in another family by birth and he may very well prefer, at least at times, to emphasize that membership rather than the voluntary relation of caring he has with you.

Before I give you the wrong impression: I wrote of unselfishness, not martyrdom on your part. Be sensible. If you think about it you know when what is being asked of you is ridiculous or impractical. You and the child are obligated to live in a real world, and so are his parents.

Do Not Play Games

You may find yourself in the middle of a disagreement between the parents and the caseworker, which results in conflict between you and the caseworker....The point is to not let yourself get caught in the middle of the biological parent and child or the biological parent and caseworker. Being honest with the parents may be a lot harder than it sounds. For one thing, it means that you cannot enter into the unreal world of planning for the impossible that some parents create. Being honest does not mean passing judgment or saying everything you think. It does mean that you will not enter into the evasions of the parent or practice them yourself. Nor should you pretend to be the parents' friend and actually be undermining their position with the child.

Of course, when even a small step is taken that may lead to growth in the parent and possible restoration of the family, it should be met with encouragement.

Support the Caseworker-Parent Relationship

For various reasons a great deal of distrust and hostility may be directed toward the caseworker by the parents. The parents' widespread resentment of the conditions of their lives is frequently directed at the agency. Many who receive much help from welfare agencies resent both the need for help and the people through whom it is delivered. The worker may be the target of resentment that has little direct connection with her actions.

In this situation, you can help by explaining to the parent the actions the caseworker takes. But do not forget you want to increase understanding, not take sides.

Possibly you can also help the caseworker understand the parent. You may have opportunity to see a side of the parent the caseworker never sees.

Never conceal from the caseworker anything you accidentally learn about the parent that will affect the child's welfare, and never agree to keep such a confidence from her. If you have ethical problems with this, remember that you are taking care of the child and your first responsibility is to the child. If the mother says, "I'll tell you something if you promise to keep it a secret," you should say, "No, I can't promise that, but I will promise to do what I think is right and what I think is best for your child..."

Do Not Overreact to Criticism

Another thing that sometimes disturbs foster parents is a tendency on the part of parents to belittle or undercut them. The foster parent must develop enough toughness and understanding to take this in stride. The specific complaint is usually petty— maybe the parent finds something to criticize about the way the child is dressed when she visits. Or in your presence the parent encourages the child to complain about his situation, and promises all this will change when she returns home.

Try to remember that the parent knows that you are doing the job she should be doing, and that merely your existence is difficult for her to accept. The less adequately she was doing the job— and the more her personal inadequacy rather than circumstances is the cause of the child's being in foster care, the more picky she may be with you. Just do not let it get under your skin— and do not take it out on the child. If it is a persistent problem, you should say quite matter-of-factly that you are doing the best you can and that her criticisms make it harder for you to help her child. I doubt if this will do much good, but it might make you feel better. I would not rebuke the mother in the child's hearing. The child may be feeling uncomfortable about the parent's complaints, and torn between two loyalties.

I do not want to imply that getting to know these parents is all problems and all giving on your part. It can be an experience that tremendously enriches your life.[105]

PRINCIPLES FOR SOCIAL WORKERS

There are many principles for social work practice. Some writers, for example, Horejsi, Bertsche, and Clark, in *Social Work Practice With Parents of Children in Foster Care*,[106] have applied these principles to working with biological parents. The medium through which the helping takes place, in working with biological parents, is the relationship. We all know that relationships elicit strong positive and negative feelings. By definition, a relationship is never neutral. As a social worker, your relationships with biological parents are developed through your communication and transactions. Positive relationships with biological parents don't just develop magically. There are principles of good social work practice that you can demonstrate with your behavior towards the parent that will increase the possibilities of developing a positive working relationship.

Biestek's classic work, *The Casework Relationship*,[107] provides the following principles to guide a social worker's helping behaviors: individualization; purposeful expression of feelings; controlled emotional involvement; acceptance; the nonjudgmental attitude; client self-determination, and confidentiality.

Individualization

We all want to be recognized as unique human beings having our own personal differences and life situations. No one wants to be considered "a case" or "a client." To individualize biological parents you must deal with your own bias and prejudice toward them as persons who have failed or hurt their children. You must have a knowledge of human behavior to understand them, be able to move at their pace, and to demonstrate the ability to enter into their feelings.

Purposeful Expression of Feelings

To establish good relationships with people, they must feel free to express both good and bad feelings if they want to. You must offer biological parents the opportunity to express themselves fully, even inviting negative feelings about you and your agency. Sometimes you can validate these feelings and admit to being a part of the problem, since workers and agencies cannot be perfect. By doing so, you permit them to relieve pressure and tension by getting these feelings off their chest, enabling them to see situations more clearly and take necessary actions. You will also get a better sense of the parents and their situations. You will have to accept anger and pain, and help them see how feelings can impair or free the actions they need to take to become more of a part of their children's lives.

Controlled Emotional Involvement

Biestek describes this principle as "the caseworker's sensitivity to the client's feelings, an understanding of their meaning, and a purposeful, appropriate response to the client's feelings."[108] As suggested earlier, the caseworker's transactions with biological parents are intrinsic to building a positive relationship. Perlman emphasizes that the professional helping "relationship is an emotional experience...if a would-be helper is to influence a [biological parent] help-seeker to cope with his problem...he will need to connect with and be responsive to the emotions with which the person's problem is charged."[109] The helping relationship is based on verbal and nonverbal communication. It is extremely important to respond to the various subjects and levels of communication with an appropriate empathic response that is sensitive and well timed.

Acceptance

Biological parents deeply want to be accepted as people of worth and inherent dignity regardless of personal problems or characteristics and past failures. A social worker must create a climate of acceptance. According to Biestek: "Acceptance does not mean approval of deviant attitudes or behavior. The object of acceptance is not 'the good' but 'the real.' The purpose of acceptance is therapeutic: to aid the caseworker in understanding the client as he really is, thus making casework more effective; and to help the client free himself from undesirable defenses, so that he feels safe to reveal himself and look at himself as he really is, and thus to deal with his problem and himself in a more realistic way."[110]

Biological parents expect that they will not be accepted and will act accordingly. We all know the saying that the best defense is a good offense! In social work we often say "accept the person but not the behavior." Easier said than done, but as people-helpers, we have to work on overcoming our own obstacles to acceptance of biological parents. Each social worker has a certain degree of skill in acceptance, and this may vary from day to day or from client to client. With growing self-awareness, our skills and attitudes can get better too. Some obstacles to acceptance are insufficient knowledge of patterns of human behavior; nonacceptance of something in yourself; imputing to the client one's own feelings; one's own biases and prejudices; unwarranted reassurances; the confusion between acceptance and approval; loss of respect for the client; and overidentification.[111]

The Nonjudgmental Attitude

No one enjoys being judged, especially if the judge does not have a relationship with the person in the position of being judged—hasn't walked that mile in his or her shoes. Biological parents of children in foster care are particularly sensitive to being judged and condemned. They usually feel that they have failed as parents (whether they say so or not) and are often full of guilt and remorse. We all know from working with biological parents that their feelings are played out in a variety of ways, many of which are very subtle. As Biestek states:

> A social worker's nonjudgmental attitude is based on a conviction that the casework function excludes assigning guilt or innocence, or degree of client

responsibility for causation of the problems or needs. This concept is misunderstood by many. It does not mean a disregard of value systems or that the worker never makes value judgments. That, of course, would be impossible. Nonjudging does not mean...that the social worker is indifferent to what the client does or says, nor does it mean that the worker condones every kind of client behavior....The worker must not judge the client but ...may assess specific behaviors and their consequences. He can help a client understand why others think that he has done "wrong" or how his behavior hurts rather than helps him or those close to him....This assessment of behavior can be in terms of its impact on goal achievement rather than in terms of right and wrong.[112]

Being nonjudgmental is especially important in the initial phase of building a relationship with biological parents, because they will fear that any information they give will be used against them. Some social workers think that the positive form of judging—praise and approval—can also cause clients to feel that they are approved of only when they show their best side.[113] We recognize that demonstrating a nonjudgmental attitude is a skill that is learned over time and with supervision.

Client Self-Determination

Engaging biological parents in building the helping relationship can seem an especially slow process at a time when permanency planning requires time limits. Active participation in the decision-making aspects of both their and their children's lives is one of the ultimate goals in working with biological parents. States Biestek:

The principle of client self-determination is the practical recognition of the right and need of clients to freedom in making their own choices and decisions in the casework process. Caseworkers have a corresponding duty to respect that right, recognize that need, stimulate and help to activate that potential for self-direction by helping the client to see and use the available and appropriate resources of the community and of his own personality. The client's right to self-determination, however, is limited by the client's capacity for positive and constructive decision making, by the framework of civil and moral law, and by the function of the agency.[114]

We can often stifle biological parents' self-determination by (1) assuming the principal responsibility for the working out of the problem and allowing the biological parents to play only a subordinate role; (2) insisting on a minute scrutinizing of the social or emotional life of the biological parents; (3) directly or indirectly manipulating the biological parents; and (4) persuading in a controlling way.[115] There are certain activities that the social worker can focus on to facilitate the biological parents' involvement in making the principle of self-determination work: (1) help the parents to see their problems or needs clearly and with perspective; (2) acquaint them with resources in their community; (3) introduce stimuli that will bring into action the parents' own dormant resources; and (4) create personal, professional, and environmental relationships with which the parents can grow and work out their problems. As Biestek's states, the role of the caseworker in client self-determination is to "open doors and windows to let in air, light, and sunshine, so that the client can breathe more easily and see more clearly. The aim is to help him gain a better insight into his problem, and develop strength to help himself."[116]

Clearly there are limitations to your facilitating biological parents' self-determination— among the biggest obstacles are large caseloads and unavailable resources. But if you are frustrated by these problems, imagine how the biological parents must feel and offer to tackle the obstacles together.

Confidentiality

The principle of confidentiality in foster care can be tricky and complex. Your responsibility is not only to the foster child but to the biological parent and foster parent. Your role and how you play it out as a mediator are critical.

Confidentiality can be defined as "the preservation of secret information concerning the client which is disclosed in the professional relationship. Confidentiality is based upon a basic right of the client; it is an ethical obligation of the caseworker and is necessary for effective casework service. The client's right, however, is not absolute. Moreover, the client's secret is often shared with other professional persons within the agency and in other agencies; the obligation then binds all equally."[117]

The issue of confidentiality must be discussed with the biological parents. They must have a clear idea as to your role as a mediator and how that influences your sharing certain information that will directly influence their relationship with the child. Although confidentiality is necessary with all people in the foster care helping relationship, the foster care triad, with its relationships to the legal system, is a most unusual configuration that warrants your working with your supervisor or other agency personnel to establish a working contract concerning confidentiality.

The principles for foster parents and social workers are not exclusive to each party. Clearly we have much to learn from one another and much overlap, but each plays a vital role in helping children and families.

6

YOU ARE NOT ALONE: THE AGENCY AS PARTNER

W e have attempted to broaden your role with the biological parents, but you are not alone in this; the agency should be right next to you, supporting you in your efforts and making major efforts on its own. You are part of the frontline team. Recognition must be given to the various parallel roles and tasks of each team member. The social worker performs the role of mediator and coordinator among the various parts of the team. As such, the social worker is available to facilitate communication between the children and their biological parents and foster parents whenever the situation warrants it. Foster parents are offering, modeling, and supporting child care skills around the clock. There are roles that only foster parents can play and roles that only the social worker can play. It is important not to take too much on yourself. It is critical for foster parents, when they are doing so much to help the family, to use the social worker and agency for support.

Foster parent Evelyn Felker says, "The agency retains responsibility for the child and delegates the care to you; the caseworker will be keeping track of the welfare of the child. She should check to see how you are doing, make inquiries about the child, be concerned with all aspects of his development. She should know the questions to ask and you should expect her to ask them and give her full answers."[118]

The caseworker also acts as the contact between the biological parents and the agency. She may be responsible for obtaining services they need, especially by placing them in contact with those that will help parents get ready to resume care of their child. She will help arrange visits within the guidelines the court or agency has set. She may even pick the child up for such visits or accompany the biological parents to the foster home.

The caseworker is also responsible for helping foster parents solve problems and for answering questions. It is not an imposition to ask for help. No one ever reaches the point of knowing all there is to know about caring for foster children, and the worker and the foster parents are continually involved in learning to do the job better. As you try to help a particular child, the worker and foster parents will be learning together.

GROUP SERVICES

The agency may also provide group services. Group services are seen as enterprises in mutual aid where persons having common concerns come and talk together to help each other. There can be groups for children, for teens, for biological parents. Social workers have meetings and so do foster parents— separately and together, creating support systems for both. Workers and foster parents have special knowledge and experience to contribute. Together they express their feelings and work on the difficult tasks of being frontline helpers to the biological parents as well as the child.

A Foster Parents' Group

To show how groups can help, here is an excerpt from a social worker's notes on a meeting of foster parents that was part of a five-session workshop on foster parenting for new foster parents, that is, those who had foster children for six months or less. Because the children were with them and the tasks were still new, the work is energetic and powerful. A social worker was present for the group, as well as an experienced foster parent who came to tell about her own experiences.

> The session began with my asking for any concerns or leftover questions from last week. One foster mother said that her foster children, placed last month after severe abuse at home, were just ordered back to their home immediately by the court. This

raised feelings of shock, fear, and concern. My responsiveness to these feelings brought forth more feeling. I also gave information on the court process, and the emotional expression that followed led us into the parent's place in the child's life. Most voiced the idea that you have to help children love their parents no matter what the parents did...I asked how real this could be to a child. One foster mother then spoke movingly of her own history, which was like our foster children's, and she has always hated her mother for deserting her. Another foster mother said she was also raised by an aunt, but she forgave her mother and knew she loved her anyway. I used the two different experiences to show how foster children may feel about their parents, stressing that the anger and bitterness of a child are hard to relate to, and foster parents may tend to sugarcoat things because of this. The value of talking to the children about their parents and allowing them to raise their own concerns was discussed by the group. One foster mother felt that she would rather wait until the child talked about it before opening it up. Another felt that her foster child had no feelings about the parent. I asked the two foster mothers who offered their own histories whether they had had feelings about their parents, and whether they were able to talk about it. Both described a longing to know about their parents and how they were not really encouraged to ask questions. I brought in the "Hidden Parent" article and the place of the parent in the child's fantasy life was discussed. Several had read the article and were able to make a connection between it and their foster child's and their own experiences.

We discussed why it is sometimes hard for foster parents to encourage talk about the parents. A great deal of anger at abusive parents was expressed here. One foster mother said, "I hate B's mother for what she did to him (scalding). I don't know how I can help him to think about her. I can't without being furious." I agreed that it is very hard to help children with something that makes oneself angry and may evoke painful memories for them. Jealousy of the child's love for this "bad mother" was also expressed and discussed. Another foster mother said angrily that "these mothers" never change. Others challenged that, however, and the experienced foster parent told how it took years, but her foster children were able to return home. The various reasons for placing children were discussed. Abuse and desertion were felt to be the most repulsive and hard to deal with in terms of helping the child deal with what they as adults could not understand. But helping the child to talk about it was now seen more as a positive than a negative, particularly since the two foster mothers who were not raised by their own mothers stressed that they wished they had had someone to talk to about it.

The mothers struggled with their feelings toward parents, and seemed open to hearing from me and from each other on the importance of opening the door for the children to talk about their parents. As we ended, Mrs. Y. said we need a whole workshop on this, and we all agreed.[119]

In this example we can see foster parents helping each other with some of the difficult aspects of dealing with the parents. The foster parents reared outside of their own homes made this work real in a way that no merely educational approach could do. The long perspective of the more experienced foster parent was helpful as well.

A Children's Group

Children, too, are often able to express their concerns more easily with other children who have experienced similar painful situations. The following are excerpts from a children's group made up of two girls and three boys, eight to ten years old, who had all been physically abused and had lived in several foster homes.

The coworkers used story telling supplemented by paper figures cut from magazines to engage the

members. The story was about the birth of a child
into a family and followed the child and the family
until the child was ten. At first the story was told by
the workers; in later sessions, the children were
encouraged to make up a story about a child and his
or her family. Even in the first session, talk about
families was accompanied by Steven repeatedly hitting a doll and by other children socking any toy
close at hand.

By the second session, as the worker's story was
repeated and members were asked to tell about the
new baby, Elizabeth looked at a picture cut from a
magazine and said, "This baby's got a black eye." (It
was a picture of an infant lying on its stomach with
the mother's hand resting on the infant's back; there
was no black eye.) When the worker wondered how
this happened, another child responded, "Someone
punched her." The children became agitated and
could not continue the story. The story was abandoned for that session and the children began to tell
of their own experiences. Kimberly began to talk of
her broken bones and the trip to the hospital when
she was found. Others, too, talked and listened to
each other. There often were only partial sentences,
and expressions of agitation and frustration were
mainly nonverbal, with body movements and hitting
and fighting among themselves. For the first time,
this group recognized a more basic common
problem...they had all been neglected and abused by
parental figures in their past.

Later, after having developed trust in the workers
and having become more at ease about their experiences, the children were ready to involve themselves
further in the story telling. The little girl in their story
was named Pamela Renee and was placed in a foster
home. They wove their story together with some of
their real-life experiences. They distinguished their
biological and foster mothers by calling them "old
mommas" and "new mommas." Kim told the other
members that they needed to pray for "old mom-

mas." Other members nodded their heads sadly. Current problems they were having with other children at school became a subject of discussion. They told each other how they answered schoolmates who asked them questions about their past and present that they really did not want to answer.

The principal theme of the group was not attended to in every session of the group, but did recur as children were able to deal with it. They were finally able to use puppets to play out a story of a family and the abuse that occurred. It seemed that these children needed to deal with thoughts and feelings about the past step-by-step.[120]

A Teen Group

The following group meeting of adolescent girls in foster care (age 16 to 18) shows the fruits of a good group services program for children and of good foster parenting. It is a final meeting of a group before the girls finished with foster care formally.

The mood was quiet, thoughtful, and very close. Leticia said with pride and determination, "This group helped me to be different. I'm the only one in my family not pregnant, and I'm the only one going to college." Kenya said, "Yeah, me too. I never thought I'd even make it out of high school. I guess I never cared either. I used to run around and mess with dope and everything. But I did those things when I had nothing better to do, now I'm gonna give college a try." Carin said softly, "Life matters more now, not always, but more. When I become a doctor I'm gonna help a lot of people." Kenya said she would be her first patient, and everyone laughed. Millie, who steadily plugged away at school, said, "No one at home thinks I can make it but I know now that I don't have to show them. Millie is going to make it for Millie!" Glenda said, "Right on!" and added, "I love college and I think I may even become a social worker. Life is great, my foster mother loves and trusts me now more than ever!" Her only complaint was that her younger sisters were in trouble and driving the family crazy— the agency ought to start a group for 11- and 12-year-olds! Everyone agreed with her, saying they could have used it too. Cherise spoke of nursing school and of moving South with her foster family. Then she added quietly, "I wish I could stay here with the group. I've changed in the group. I've grown from hate into kindness."[121]

Cherise was speaking of an increased ability to love herself and others because she experienced love through the efforts of the worker, the group, and her foster family.

The agency provides a range of services to support foster parents, biological parents, and children. Group services, which empower group members to harness their strengths in pursuit of common tasks, are particularly effective. The agency needs feedback from foster parents and workers about what services and resources are needed. You have walked the miles, you know the terrain, your suggestions can be very helpful.

Foster parents' input into the process of helping foster children and their family is critical. Foster parents see a side of each that social workers usually do not see. Their observations of the parent-child relationship and the strengths and weaknesses of each can enrich and deepen the helping plan. Foster parents help the children and their families as children's caregiver, a role model, a nurturer, and support system. Working together, foster parents, biological parents, social workers, and the agency will then be able to move toward the best possible permanent plan for foster children and toward preserving vital ties.

NOTES

1. Theodore Stein, "Foster Care for Children," in *Encyclopedia of Social Work*, vol. 1, ed. Anne Minahan, (Silver Spring, MD: National Association of Social Workers, 1987), 639.

2. *Ibid.*

3. *Ibid.*

4. Carel B. Germain, ed., *Social Work Practice: People and Environments* (New York: Columbia University Press, 1979), 1–22, and Carel B. Germain and Alex Gitterman, *The Life Model of Social Work Practice* (New York: Columbia University Press, 1980).

5. Germain, *Social Work Practice*, and Germain and Gitterman, *The Life Model.*

6. A.N. Maluccio, E. Fein, and K.A. Olmstead, *Permanency Planning for Children: Concepts and Methods* (New York: Tavistock Publications, 1986).

7. Stein, "Foster Care for Children," 645.

8. "God Bless The Child..." *Hartford Courant,* March 19, 1988; Andrew Stein, "Children of Poverty: Crisis In New York," *The New York Times Magazine,* June 8, 1986; Kathleen Megan, "The American Nightmare: Homeless on $356 a Week," *Northeast Magazine* (November 27, 1988): 18–23.

9. Stein, "Foster Care for Children," 645.

10. *Ibid.*, 641.

11. A.N. Maluccio and E. Fein, "Growing Up in Foster Care," *Children and Youth Service Review* 7 (February–March 1985): 123–134.

12. "Child Abuse and Neglect Rocketed 150% in Reagan Years," *Child Protection Report* 14, 12 (June 10, 1988): 1,4, 5.

13. Michael Oreskes, "The System Overloaded: The Foster-Care Crisis," *The New York Times* (March 15, 1987): 1, 32, and S.M. Rosen, D. Fanshel, and M.E. Lutz, (ed.).

14. E. Milling Kinard, "Child Abuse and Neglect," in *Encylopedia of Social Work*, Volume 1, ed. Anne Minahan, (Silver Spring, MD: National Association of Social Workers, 1987), 226, and Child Protection Report.

15. Kinard, "Child Abuse and Neglect," 226.

16. Joan Laird, "An Ecological Approach to Child Welfare: Issues of Family Identity and Continuity," in *Social Work Practice: People and Environment*, ed. Carel B. Germain, (New York: Columbia University Press, 1979), 204.

17. Charles Levy, *Social Work Ethics*, (New York: Human Science Press, 1976), 113.

18. A.N. Maluccio, "Foster Family Care Revisited: Problems and Prospects," *Public Welfare* 31 (Spring 1973): 12.

19. Levy, *Social Work Ethics*, 112.

20. William Schwartz, "The Social Worker in the Group," in *The Practice of Group Work*, ed. Robert Klenk and Robert Ryan (California: Wadsworth Publishing Company, 1974), 208–228.

21. *Ibid.*

22. Maluccio, Fein, and Olmstead, *Permanency Planning for Children*, 67.

23. Germain and Gitterman, *The Life Model.*

24. Maluccio, Fein, and Olmstead, *Permanency Planning for Children.*

25. Jean Charnley, *The Art of Child Placement* (Minneapolis, MN: University of Minnesota Press, 1955), 114.

26. Evelyn Felker, *Foster Parenting Young Children—Guidelines from a Foster Parent* (New York: Child Welfare League of America, 1974), 63–65.

27. Stein, "Foster Care for Children," 640.

28. *Ibid.*

29. *Ibid.*, 640-641.

30. Alfred Kadushin, *Child Welfare Services*, 3rd ed. (New York: Macmillian Publishing Company, 1980), 349.

31. Peg Hess and Kathleen Proch, *Family Visiting in Out-of-Home Care: A Guide to Practice* (Washington, DC: Child Welfare League of America, 1988), 11–25.

32. Laird, "An Ecological Approach to Child Welfare," 175–176.

33. Lela Costin, *Child Welfare: Policies and Practice* (New York: McGraw-Hill Book Co., 1979), 243.

34. Committee On Ways and Means, U.S. House of Representatives, *"Background Material and Data on Programs Within the Jurisdiction of the Committee on Ways and Means"* (Washington, DC: U .S. Government Printing Office, March 24, 1988), 594.

35. Laird, "An Ecological Approach to Child Welfare," 179.

36. Judith A.B. Lee, "Promoting Competence In Children and Youth" in *Promoting Competence In Clients: An Old/New Approach,* ed. A.N. Maluccio (Glencoe, IL: The Free Press, 1981), 237.

37. Stein, "Foster Care for Children," 641.

38. Shirley Jenkins and Mignon Sauber, *Paths to Child Placement* (New York: The Community Council of Greater New York, 1966), 62.

39. *Ibid.*, 61–62.

40. Felker, *Foster Parenting Young Children,* 67.

41. Jenkins and Sauber, *Paths to Child Placement,* 82–83.

42. *Ibid.,* 103–105.

43. *Ibid.,* 123, 134.

44. Ray E. Helfer and C. Henry Kempe, eds., *The Battered Child* (Chicago, IL: The University of Chicago Press, 1974).

45. Kathleen Coulborn Faller,ed., *Social Work With Abused and Neglected Children* (New York: The Free Press, 1981), 20.

46. Ruth S. and C. Henry Kempe, *Child Abuse* (Cambridge, MA: Harvard University Press, 1978), 7.

47. Faller, *Social Work with Abused and Neglected Children,* 18.

48. Jan R. Conte, "Child Sexual Abuse," in Encyclopedia of Social Work, Volume 1, ed. Anne Minahan (Silver Spring, MD: National Association of Social Workers, 1987), 257.

49. Faller, *Social Work with Abused and Neglected Children,* 17.

50. The National Center on Child Abuse and Neglect, *A Curriculum on Child Abuse and Neglect: Leader's Manual* (Washington, DC: U.S. Department of Health, Education and Welfare, September 1979), 153.

51. Faller, *Social Work with Abused and Neglected Children*, 37.

52. Oreskes, "The System Overloaded," 1, 32.

53. Faller, *Social Work with Abused and Neglected Children*, 37.

54. Jenkins and Sauber, *Paths to Child Placement*, 160.

55. *Ibid.*, 161–162.

56. Rosina M. Becerra and Eve P. Fielder, "Adolescent Pregnancy," in *Encyclopedia of Social Work*, vol. 1, ed. Ann Minahan, (Silver Spring, MD: National Association of Social Workers, 1987), 46–47.

57. Donal M. Loppnow, "Adolescents on Their Own," in *A Handbook of Child Welfare*, ed. Joan Laird and Ann Hartman, (New York: The Free Press, 1985), 529.

58. Albert G. Crawford and Frank F. Furstenberg, Jr., "Teenage Sexuality, Pregnancy, and Childbearing," in *A Handbook of Child Welfare*, ed. Joan Laird and Ann Hartman, (New York: The Free Press, 1985).

59. *Ibid.*, 544–45.

60. *Ibid.*, and Ruth J. Parsons, "Empowerment for Role Alternatives for Low-Income Minority Girls: A Group Work Approach," in *Group Work With the Poor and Oppressed*, ed. Judith A.B. Lee, (Haworth Press, in press).

61. Parsons, "Empowerment for Role Alternatives."

62. Loppnow, "Adolescents on Their Own."

63. Ner Littner, "The Art of Being a Foster Parent," *Child Welfare* LVII, 1 (January 1978): 12.

64. *Ibid.*, 7–8.

65. Felker, *Foster Parenting Young Children*, 63.

66. Shirley Jenkins and Elaine Norman. *Filial Deprivation and Foster Care* (New York: Columbia University Press, 1972), 266.

67. Phyllis McAdams, "The Parents in the Shadows," *Child Welfare* LI, 1 (January 1972): 51–55.

68. Child Welfare League of America, "Introduction to Foster Parenting" (New York: Child Welfare League of America, 1976) Film Transcript, and "Don't Condemn Me Till You Know Me," (Washington, DC: U.S. Department of Health, Education and Welfare, 1976).

69. Carol Swenson, "Social Networks, Mutual Aid, and the Life Model of Practice," in *Social Work Practice: People and Environments*, ed. Carel B. Germain, (New York: Columbia Free Press, 1979), 213–235.

70. Ann Hartman, "Diagrammatic Assessment of Family Relationships," *Social Casework* (October, 1978): 465–476.

71. *Ibid.*, 467-469, 471.

72. *Ibid.*, p. 471.

73. Monica McGoldrick, John K. Pearce, and Joseph Giordano, eds. *Ethnicity and Family Therapy* (New York: The Guilford Press, 1982), 4.

74. *Ibid.*

75. Shirley Jenkins and Beverly Diamond, "Ethnicity and Foster Care: Census Data As Predictors of Placement Variables," *American Journal of Orthopsychiatry* 55, 2 (April 1985): 267–276.

76. William Roth, "Disabilities: Physical," in *Encyclopedia of Social Work*, vol. 1, ed. Ann Minahan, (Silver Spring, MD: National Association of Social Workers, 1987), 434–38.

77. Rosemary Haraguchi, "Adolescent Self-Image: A Roadmap to Destiny," in *The Handicapped Child and His Family*, ed. D. Gitler and D. Vigliaroco (New York: New York University Medical Center, Institute For Rehabilitative Medicine, Medical Research Monograph, 1978), 17–32.

78. Aimee McDonnell, "A Social Work Perspective On the Handicapped Child and His Family," 55–71.

79. "AIDS: We Need to Know. We Need to Care" (Silver Spring, MD: National Association of Social Workers). A public service campaign pamphlet. This information is also contained in "The Surgeon General's Report on AIDS" (Washington, DC: U.S. Department of Health and Human Services, 1987).

80. Terence Monmanley, "Kids With AIDS," *Newsweek* (September 7, 1987): 51–59.

81. *Ibid.*

82. George Getzel and Diego Lopez, "Strategies for Volunteers Caring For Person's With AIDS," *Social Casework* (January 1987): 53.

83. George Getzel, *AIDS and Families* (New York: Gay Men's Health Crisis Publication, 1987).

84. Agnes B. Hatfield and Harriet P. Lefley, *Families of the Mentally Ill: Coping and Adaptation* (New York: The Guilford Press, 1987), 9–15.

85. Lynn McDonald-Wikler, "Disabilities: Developmental," in *Encyclopedia of Social Work*, vol. I, ed. Anne Minahan, (Silver Spring, MD: National Association of Social Workers, 1987), 422–433.

86. Hatfield and Lefley, *Families of The Mentally Ill*, 9–15, and McDonald-Wikler, "Disabilities: Developmental," 422–433.

87. Hilda Hidalgo, Travis L. Peterson, and Natalie Jane Woodman, eds. *Lesbian and Gay Issues: A Resource Manual For Social Workers* (Silver Spring, MD: National Association of Social Workers, 1985), 13.

88. A. Elfin Moses and Robert O. Hawkins, Jr. *Counseling Lesbian Woman and Gay Men: A Life-Issues Approach* (St. Louis, MO: The C.V. Mosby Co., 1982),15.

89. For a definition of homophobia and other terms used here, please see Hidalgo, Peterson, and Woodman, eds., *Lesbian and Gay Issues*, 8–9.

90. *Ibid.*, 9.

91. Moses and Hawkins, *Counseling Lesbian Woman and Gay Men*, 198.

92. *Ibid.*, 198–200.

93. *Ibid.*, 90.

94. Littner, "The Art of Being a Foster Parent," 13.

95. Child Welfare League of America, "Introduction to Foster Parenting."

96. Charnley, *The Art of Child Placement*, 109.

97. Almeda Jolowicz, "The Hidden Parent," in Sourcebook of Teaching Materials on the Welfare of Children (New York: Council on Social Work Education, 1969), 105–107.

98. Judith A.B. Lee and Danielle N. Park, "A Group Work Approach to the Depressed Adolescent Girl in Foster Care," *American Journal of Orthopsychiatry* 48,3 (July 1978): 521.

99. Felker, Foster Parenting Young Children, 61–62.

100. Linda J. Davies and David C. Bland, "The Use of Foster Parents as Role Models for Parents," *Child Welfare* LVII, 6 (June 1978): 380–386.

101. Charnley, The Art of Child Placement, 164.

102. Davies and Bland, "The Use of Foster Parents as Role Models for Parents," 384.

103. Patricia Ryan, Emily Jean McFadden, and Bruce L. Warren, "Foster Families: A Resource for Helping Parents," in *The Challenge of Partnership: Working With Parents of Children in Foster Care*, ed. Anthony Maluccio and Paula A. Sinanoglu (New York: Child Welfare League of America, Inc., 1981), 189–199.

104. Swenson, "Social Networks, Mutual Aid, and the Life Model of Practice," and Swenson, "Using Natural Helping Networks to Promote Competence," in *Promoting Competence in Clients - An Old/New Approach*, ed. A. N. Maluccio (Glencoe, IL: The Free Press, 1981).

105. Felker, Foster Parenting Young Children, 63–67.

106. Charles R. Horejsi, Anne Vandeberg Bertsche, and Frank W. Clark, *Social Work Practice With Parents of Children in Foster Care* (Springfield, IL: Charles C. Thomas Publisher, 1981).

107. Felix P. Biestek, Jr., *The Casework Relationship* (Chicago, IL: Loyola University Press, 1957).

108. *Ibid.*, 50.

109. Horejsi, Bertsche, and Clark, *Social Work Practice With Parents of Children in Foster Care*, 54.

110. Biestek, *The Casework Relationship*, 72.

111. *Ibid.*, 81–87.

112. Horejsi, Bertsche, and Clark, *Social Work Practice With Parents of Children in Foster Care*, 55.

113. Biestek, *The Casework Relationship*, 103.

114. *Ibid.*, 106–107.

115. *Ibid.*, 105–107.

116. *Ibid.*, 106.

117. *Ibid.*, 121.

118. Felker, *Foster Parenting Young Children*, 49–50.

119. For further discussion of this approach to foster parents' workshop and groups, see Judith A.B. Lee, "The Foster Parents Workshop: A Social Work Approach to Learning For New Foster Parents," *Social Work With Groups* 2, 2 (Summer 1979): 129–143.

120. Marian Fatout, "Group Work with Severely Abused and Neglected Latency Age Children: Social Needs and Problems," *Social Work with Groups* 10, 4 (Winter 1987): 5–19.

121. Lee and Park, "A Group Work Approach to the Depressed Adolescent Girl in Foster Care," 525.

ABOUT THE AUTHORS

Judith A.B. Lee, D.S.W., is a Professor of Social Work and Casework Chairperson at the University of Connecticut School of Social Work. Dr. Lee worked for ten years as a practitioner and administrator in New York City's Bureau of Child Welfare, Division of Foster Home Care and Adoptive Services. Her current social work practice is with homeless women and children in Hartford. A nationally known scholar, Dr. Lee has a book and 23 chapters and articles to her credit. She is also president of the Association for the Advancement of Social Work with Groups, an international professional organization.

Danielle Nisivoccia, D.S.W., is Acting Deputy Director and Director of Curriculum Development at the James Satterwhite Child Welfare Training Academy in New York City. She is also adjunct Associate Professor at New York University and Yeshiva University Schools of Social Work. Dr. Nisivoccia has practiced, supervised, administered, taught and written in the field of child welfare for over 17 years. She is committed to providing quality services to strengthen families.